Quick & Easy Activities

for 4th–6th Graders

Zondervan/Youth Specialties Books

Adventure Games
Amazing Tension Getters
Attention Grabbers for 4th-6th Graders (Get 'Em Growing)
Called to Care
The Complete Student Missions Handbook
Creative Socials and Special Events
Divorce Recovery for Teenagers
Feeding Your Forgotten Soul
Get 'Em Talking
Good Clean Fun
Good Clean Fun, Volume 2
Great Games for 4th-6th Graders (Get 'Em Growing)
Great Ideas for Small Youth Groups
Greatest Skits on Earth
Greatest Skits on Earth, Volume 2
Growing Up in America
High School Ministry
High School TalkSheets
Holiday Ideas for Youth Groups (Revised Edition)
Hot Talks
Ideas for Social Action
Intensive Care: Helping Teenagers in Crisis
Junior High Ministry
Junior High TalkSheets
The Ministry of Nurture
On-Site: 40 On-Location Programs for Youth Groups
Option Plays
Organizing Your Youth Ministry
Play It! Great Games for Groups
Quick and Easy Activities for 4th-6th Graders (Get 'Em Growing)
Teaching the Bible Creatively
Teaching the Truth about Sex
Tension Getters
Tension Getters II
Unsung Heroes: How to Recruit and Train Volunteer Youth Workers
Up Close and Personal: How to Build Community in Your Youth Group
Youth Ministry Nuts & Bolts
Youth Specialties Clip Art Book
Youth Specialties Clip Art Book, Volume 2

Quick & Easy Activities

for 4th–6th Graders

DAVID LYNN

Youth Specialties

ZondervanPublishingHouse
Grand Rapids, Michigan

A Division of HarperCollinsPublishers

Disclaimer

Like life, this book contains activities that, in an unfortunate combination of circumstances, could result in emotional or physical harm. Before you use a game, you'll need to evaluate it on its own merit for your group, for its potential risk, for necessary safety precautions and advance preparation, and for possible results. Youth Specialties, Inc., Zondervan Publishing House, and David Lynn are not responsible for, nor have they any control over, the use or misuse of any games published in this book.

Quick and Easy Activities for 4th-6th Graders Copyright © 1990 by Youth Specialties, Inc.

Youth Specialties Books, 1224 Greenfield Drive, El Cajon, California 92021, are published by Zondervan Publishing House, 1415 Lake Drive, S.E., Grand Rapids, Michigan 49506

Library of Congress Cataloging-in-Publication Data

Lynn, David, 1954-
    Quick and easy activities for 4th-6th graders : fantastic meeting starters, teaching activities, and special events to spark your 8-to-12-year-olds / David Lynn.
        p.   cm.
        "Get 'em growing from Youth Specialties."
        "Zondervan/Youth Specialties books"—P.
        ISBN 0-310-52551-9
        1. Group games. 2. Games in Christian education. I. Title. II. Title: Quick and easy activities for fourth through sixth graders.
    GV1203.L95 1990
    794—dc20

90-38499
CIP

Edited by Kathy George
Designed by Jack Rogers
Illustrations by Dan Pegoda
Typography by Leah Perry

Printed in the United States of America

90 91 92 93 94 95 96 97 98 99 /   / 10 9 8 7 6 5 4 3 2 1

To
my wife Kathy,
a co-worker and co-heir in Christ (1 Peter 3:7)

Table of Contents

Acknowledgments

The ideas found in this collection are presented as a compilation of a wide variety of activities suitable for the upper elementary grades. Many of these activities originally appeared in the *Ideas* Library published by Youth Specialties, Inc. The author would like to thank all of the creative people responsible for developing and testing the activities in this book. Without their dedication to young people, this book of quick and easy-to-do ideas would not have been possible.

David Lynn

How to Use This Book

Quick & Easy Activities for 4th–6th Graders is designed to be a useful and handy resource. It isn't meant to be a substitute for good planning, but it can offer new ideas and options for those inevitable occasions when the immediate need is for an easy-to-do meeting starter, an emergency teaching activity, or a special event that can be planned quickly. Ministering to young people always entails heavy work loads and this book is meant to help those who wish to maintain their commitment to high-quality ministry but who readily realize that there will always be times when activity ideas are needed in a hurry.

The activities in this book can all be done with upper elementary aged young people. These children are growing and changing rapidly and any activities planned for them should take these changes into consideration. Mental skills and abilities are beginning to be refined. Physical speed and endurance are increasing. Imagination and creativity are expanding. Socially, these kids are very interested in working together as a group, collaborating with peers and adults to achieve common goals. Interest in team activities and competition intensifies at the same time.

Selecting the Right Activities for Your Group

Simply because kids are interested in playing games and participating in activities does not, however, mean that just any game or activity will do. The following guidelines should be kept in mind when selecting any activities for a group of young people.

Decide upon a purpose. Before choosing any activity from this book you must have a purpose for the intended activity. Picking activities for activity's sake can be disastrous. Think through what it is that you want to accomplish before you choose any activity, game, or event. Here are the kinds of activities you will find in this book to help you meet your purposes.

• *No-Prep Games*. Games included here require little or no preparation. Any number of them are sure to become group favorites, ones that your kids will want to play again and again.

• *Easy-to-Do Meeting Starters*. Here you will find a wide variety of fun, creatively entertaining, and engaging crowd breakers that are certain to grab your kids' attention.

• *Emergency Teaching Activities*. These minimum-preparation teaching activities are ideal for on-the-spot lessons or discussions.

• *Teaching Energizers*. Designed to enhance your teaching, many of these creative activities manage to challenge your young audience and entertain them at the same time.

• *Faith Sparkers*. Here you will find a number of special activities structured to promote young people's understanding of God and to strengthen their relationship to him.

• *Quick-Plan Special Events*. Some are wild and some are crazy. They are all sure to transform a social or fellowship activity into a memorable event.

• *Ready-to-Use Growth Games*. Learning games are great ways for kids to have fun while discovering more about God's Word and the Christian life. The selection of games provided here can help kids to consider their own needs for Christian growth.

Involve your group members in the choice. Young people need to make programming decisions in partnership with adults. This does not mean that adult leaders abdicate their adult responsibilities in favor of kids making all the decisions. Rather, it is young people and adults choosing together the kinds of activities they both wish to do with each other.

Include all group members. Don't let the "personality trap" dictate your choice of activities. Consider the needs of all the kids in your group. Leaders often choose activities and games that the popular, sharp-looking, athletic kids like. These personality kids then become the litmus test for an activity's success or failure. The best bet is to select a wide variety of activities for your program. Give each person in your group opportunities to be in on the planning, to select a favorite activity, or to help with leading a discussion.

Maintain final authority. Not every activity found in this book is right for your particular group. Use ideas that fit your group's particular personality, locale, size, space, and age range. You are the final authority when it comes to selecting the events and activities in which your group will participate. You know your group of young people. It is ultimately up to you to make the decision as to which activities are or are not appropriate for your group. Just because an activity is printed in a book does not mean it is suitable or safe *for your group*.

The activities found in this book are not cast in concrete. You can adapt, change, or do whatever you need to do to make these activities work for your group. In fact, you are wise to carefully evaluate any packaged programming ideas you may purchase for your children's ministry, always feeling free to adapt them to meet your particular needs.

A Special Word About Fun and Games

Since many of the activities done with this age group involve play and fun, the following insights are offered to help guide you in your fun and game experiences with fourth, fifth, and sixth graders.

"It's not whether you win or lose, it's how you play the game"—or so we've heard. But somewhere along the way, "how you play the game" was lost. Yet how the game is played is why games need to be played. Recapturing this attitude of play is difficult. The following tips can help you restore a playful attitude within your group.

Be patient with children (and adults) who do not know how to have fun playing a game. Being "cool" requires a certain aloofness that prohibits some from having fun. Others are so preoccupied with winning that they lose the joy of play. Your group may not readily embrace a new philosophy of play. Be willing to give them time and many play experiences in order to lose the "cool" or jock image.

Young people learn more from watching you than from listening to you. A new attitude towards fun and games will more likely be caught than taught. That means you must start with changing the way adults in your group view games. If your adult leaders sit on the sidelines while expecting the kids to play, then your young people will likely opt out of playing at any excuse. If your adults push the kids to win, your games will be tense and competitive. If, however, adults who work with children jump into the fun, their excitement will be contagious. When the adults stand along the sidelines, grab their hands and pull

them into play. And when they go overboard with competition, gently remind them the purpose of play is not winning but celebrating by playing.

Competition is not bad; it's the kind *of competition that you need to monitor.* The most appropriate games involve unskilled competition—competition that requires skills that challenge all the players, not just the athletic types. Choose games that require dexterity as well as raw speed, thinking as well as reacting, subjective as well as objective responses. Games that give all the players an equal chance at winning allow everyone to have fun, not just the winners. You know you have healthy competition when the kids forget about keeping score. Structure games to equalize the competition, giving all players an equal chance to participate and succeed. At this age in particular, this is vital!

Choose games for this age group that build self-esteem. Avoid ending a game with a traditional winner (the one on top) and losers (those at the bottom). Structure the winning and losing around team efforts and present the whole team with any awards. Team winning makes it easier for the whole group to feel good about playing. (Be sure the award can be shared by all the team.) As your group experiences games that teach this new attitude of playing for fun, they will apply it when playing games that are traditionally competitive as well. Even the jock types can learn to want everyone to succeed and to play for the sheer enjoyment of play.

Explain games clearly and quickly. When introducing a game to your group, you first must have everyone's attention. This can be done by first extending an invitation for everyone to play. Give people a choice. Then use the following tips to get the game started:

- Assure players, through your gestures and tone of voice, that the game will be fun and will build them up.
- Explain and demonstrate the game in a way that all the players can hear you and see your face. Confusion during the game's explanation will frustrate kids before you even start playing.
- Tell the kids the name of the game, explain step-by-step how to play, and then demonstrate the game with another player or players.
- Show your excitement about playing the game—be a little wild and crazy. If playing the game is fun, why not make the presentation of the game fun as well? Your play attitude is contagious. Use the KISMIF principle: Keep it simple; make it fun.
- Lead the kids in a practice round of the game. This reassures the group that you want to focus on having fun rather than winning/losing. A trial run also builds trust in the play process and in the group.
- Don't take the game so seriously that you get angry with players for not getting the rules. Let your irritation signal you to move on to another game or activity.
- If the game you are explaining requires teams, divide the group before you explain the rules. If the game requires a circle, circle up before presenting the game. This makes it easier to move from the explanation to the demonstration to the practice round and finally into the game itself.

Choosing Your Play Area

A suitable place for play is as important as the right games. The most important consideration is, of course, safety. Use common sense when selecting a play area. Clear outdoor play areas of rocks, sticks, glass, and other potentially dangerous objects and debris. If the area is suitable except for a little pothole or two, cover them with a Frisbee and point them out to the group. Large holes, protruding sprinkler heads, trees, or other permanent, hazardous objects mean you must find a different play area.

Keep an indoor play area away from windows, stairways, and furniture. Clear the area of dangerous objects or obstacles. Choose only those games that can be safely played in an area the size of yours. Some games designed for large, outdoor spaces just aren't fun to play in a confined area.

Safety First
(and Second and Third)

Thinking about safety is a must for every game leader. Common sense will help you select a game, choose equipment, decide on a place to play, line up adult supervision, and actually play the game. A good rule of thumb: If it doesn't feel safe, assume it's not safe and don't play!

Vitally important to safely playing any game are the *Safety Guards*. A Safety Guard is a referee plus. Some Safety Guards referee the games, some lead the games, and others participate in play. Safety Guards are given ultimate authority when it comes to running a game. If they see play getting out of hand, they can call a time-out. If a player is participating irresponsibly, a Safety Guard can talk one-on-one with that player about safety. Safety Guards need to be prepared for their role; asking them to read this chapter is a good start.

Although Safety Guards are usually adults, kids can also act as Safety

Guards. Designate a different young person as a Safety Guard for each game you play. Rotating the responsibility around the group helps your kids recognize their personal responsibility for safety. Players will take safety more seriously if they have been in the role of Safety Guard.

Insure the safety of your players and leaders by first playing the game yourself or at least watching as it's played. If you cannot either watch it or play it, get a group of your Safety Guards together and play the game. This helps you to know what to look for while playing the game with your kids. It's crucial to preview the game to look at as many safety angles as possible. Then when you teach the kids how to play it, you can include safety cautions with your directions.

The following safety checks can help you and your Safety Guards create a safe and fun playing experience:

- *Boundary check.* Clearly mark boundaries of play and point out the boundaries to the players. If you have not clearly pointed out and marked the playing area when playing Bedlam (page 19), for example, the players could bump into something that may cause an injury.
- *Hazards check.* Remove debris and repair or mark other hazards in the playing area. Players need to remove watches, jewelry, pencils, or anything else they are wearing with which they could hurt themselves or others during play.
- *Rules check.* State the object of the game and explain its rules step-by-step. Play a practice round to observe if all the players know how to play. Too often players will nod their heads, indicating they understand the rules without really comprehending them.

Play more than one practice round, if necessary. Players entering the game should first be checked out by a Safety Guard.

- *Break check.* All players should be allowed a personal time-out any time during play. It is imperative that players feel physically and psychologically safe while playing. Players out of breath or feeling threatened by a game need the option to walk away from play. At any time during the game a player can yell, "Break time. Stop!" and play will immediately stop. This offers an immediate out to injured or exhausted players. Explain the time-out and break-time rules before each play event occurs.
- *Safety Guard check.* Are there enough Safety Guards for this game to be safe? Have the Safety Guards been prepared for their roles? These are two questions the game leader must ask himself before play. (By the way, don't play without Safety Guards just because a game in this book does not mention using them.)

Creating Play

Play does not just happen—it is created. Game leaders must create an environment where an attitude of play can flourish.

Consider that players are number one. Players are the reasons you are playing. Don't allow a game to own the players. Empower players with the attitude and skills to own a game. Flexibility is the key. Don't feel locked into strict adherence to a prescribed way of playing a game.

Involve Adults. Young people need to see adults having fun. All too often young people play games with an adult leader while the rest of the adult workers talk to each other on the sidelines.

Plan for the unexpected. Weather, group mood, and attendance are only three of the myriad surprises for a game leader. If you are planning an outdoor event, prepare a few backup indoor games in case of rain, sleet, hail, or gloom of night. As unpredictable as the weather is the mood and interest of your group. What works with your kids one month may not work the next. Plan extra games to spark their interest if things begin to slow down. Be ready for a smaller or larger group than you expected. Either bring a backup set of games for both large and small groups, or be prepared to modify the games you have chosen.

Timing is everything. Let the energy level and fun level of your kids determine how long to play a game. End a game while players are still having fun. If you keep playing until they lose interest, they will remember the boredom rather than the fun of the game. But don't end games so soon that kids feel they didn't have a chance to have fun. Use time to add excitement or lift tension in a game. In some games shortening the time limit hypes kids to play wholeheartedly. If you notice kids looking overwhelmed or frustrated, however, give them more time to do their action.

There are no such things as official rules. The only rules that should be strictly enforced are the ones that affect safety. Young people in the fourth, fifth, and sixth grades are learning the flexibility and relativity of rules, a skill foundational to more complex learning. Giving children the opportunity to change the rules or create new rules is healthy. At this age one child will say, "Last one to the house is it," and a second child retorts with, "Not included!" The first child then yells back, "No say-backs." This is an example of children using their new-found ability to manipulate rules—all part of normal, healthy development.

Changing the rules or creating new ones is also a great way to energize a game. By modifying rules players are actually creating a new game. Point out to players that when they change rules and modify games they are taking charge of creating their own play. To keep the playing happy, though, rule changes need to be agreed upon as a group before play begins.

A New Attitude Toward Winning and Losing

Many games have winners and losers, and in most games some players will do better than others. But as a game leader, you can help redefine and refocus the win/lose concept by leading your kids to evaluate their game times, by choosing team games, by using untraditional scoring methods, by choosing games that include non-athletic skills, and by making your Safety Guards your partners in changing old attitudes of competition.

Take advantage of teachable moments that sometimes follow play events to process what happened during the games. Discuss with the group what they learned from the play experience and how they felt about the competition. Lead them to remember the times during the games when certain players did their best—even if those players did not end up winning. By verbally recognizing non-winners who either improved or tried their hardest, you help kids learn to enjoy personal stretching rather than proving they are better than everyone else. (Don't try to evaluate every play experience, however.)

Another way to redefine winning and losing is by emphasizing team rather than individual competition. Team winning is different than individual victory because it requires cooperation among the team members to win. And the team that does not win does so as a team, avoiding the focus on one player either winning or not winning. When you discuss with the kids their views on competition, avoid using the word *loser*.

Scoring is another means of refocusing the win/lose concept. Traditionally scoring has had the effect of focusing play on the outcome; who wins and who loses. When this is the case with a group of kids, discontinue keeping score. You can create a new challenge and a whole new spirit to game playing by changing the way you score. Begin to give points for things players wouldn't expect. Traditionally points are awarded for the swiftest and the most, but you can give points for the funniest, the most creative, or for cooperation. Doing this also generates new enthusiasm for playing the game, especially when a game begins to slow. Make sure you include the players when you want to create a new scoring system. Train your players to look for new ways to score the games you play.

Random Scores

Next time your group is having competition between teams in several events and you want to "neutralize" things so that no team is able to dominate the other teams, here's a way to hand out points that narrows the gap. Before the competition begins, determine the point value for each event. Make sure you have enough points so that every team will receive points following every event. (For example, if you have five teams, you need at least five point entries—10, 8, 6, 4, 2.) Make up a board for each event like the illustration below, and scramble the points so that they are in no particular order.

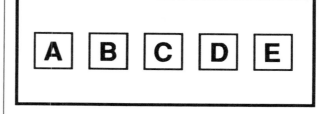

Then cover the points with construction paper squares with a letter on each one, like so:

Following every event, the points are awarded this way: The team that comes in first gets *first choice* of the letters on the board. They receive the number of points written underneath the letter they chose. Their score is purely chance, but they do get to choose first. The second place team chooses second, and so on. Sometimes the last place team actually gets the most points because no one knows how many points lie behind each letter. The first place team is generally satisfied with the privilege of choosing first, even though in the end the scores are determined by luck. Not only does this keep the competition close, but watching teams choose their letters adds extra suspense. Remember, you will need to make up a different board for each event.

Scoring can also be changed by giving away 10 points or 100 points to the placing teams or individuals. Kids will want to play their best when they can get 100 or 1000 points (who wants to play for one point?). Keep the spread between points small so that the last place team or person is still fairly close to the first place. For example, with three teams, first place may be 500 points, second place 475, and third place 450. That way the team in last still gets lots of points and has achieved something.

Also remember unskilled competition when trying to create a new attitude toward winners and losers. If kids know they can compete successfully because different kinds of skills are required, they'll not only be more eager to play but their idea of who is a winner changes.

Finally, Safety Guards can help you redefine the win/lose attitude. Train your Safety Guards to referee events in such a way that competition is equalized. They can do this by focusing more intently on infractions of the winning teams or individuals and go easier on whoever is behind. The players will soon realize that the Safety Guards are always taking the side of the underdog. After a while players will focus more on having fun than on earning points or keeping score.

No-Prep Games

Games included here require little or no preparation. Any number of them are sure to become group favorites, ones that your kids will want to play again and again.

The object of this game is for the person who is "It" to give animal identities to each of the other players without getting caught. Before starting, secretly select one person to be "It." This can be done by asking all of the players to sit down with their heads bowed and their eyes closed. Then walk among the group and designate one of the players as "It" with a silent touch on the top of the head.

Play begins with the entire group walking around the room, talking with each other and shaking each other's hands. The individual who is "It" mingles casually, attempting to give each player the name of an animal to imitate without anyone noticing. Once given an identity, players continue to mingle for a time, but must then imitate the voices of their animal identities and continue to make their animal noises throughout the rest of the game period. Players with animal identities must not draw attention to the person who is "It." Play continues until someone recognizes "It" or until "It" has successfully managed to give every player an animal identity.

Players who think that they can identify "It" can venture a guess by shouting

"Abracadabra" and pointing to the suspected player. Any players who make incorrect guesses must remove themselves from the game area for one minute of play. A special "doghouse" area can be designated for such purposes. It should be a spot away from play where the ongoing game cannot be observed. After a minute, players may rejoin the game. If a guess is correct, the round is over. Should the group wish to play again, a new "It" can be selected in the same manner as before.

Amoeba Lift

This game can be a competition between teams or it can be a cooperative game with the entire group trying to break its own record. Teams should be of equal size and should not contain more than fifteen members.

Each team becomes an "Amoeba." The amoeba has to develop a strategy whereby the entire group can be lifted up, while standing on as few legs as possible. The amoeba must stand in place for a minimum of ten seconds. Any legs that touch down during that time will be counted. Several leaders or Safety Guards should be available to help count legs during the "lift" and to help pick up the pieces when everyone falls down. The amoeba that is able to lift itself on the fewest legs is the winner.

Anatomy Clumps

Play begins with the participants milling around the room and the leader standing somewhere in the middle. After a few seconds, the leader blows a whistle and yells out the name of a body part and a number. Players then rush to get into groups of whatever number was called and to connect with each other whatever body part was called. For example, after the call "Elbow! Three!" players gather in groups of three and touch elbows. The last group to correctly follow the commands is eliminated from the game. The game continues until only one group is left and is declared the winner.

Examples of possible combinations: knee (4), nose (3), ankle (6), back (2), rear (5), neck (2), shoulder (6), and head (4).

Bedlam

This game requires four teams of equal size. Each team takes one corner of the room or playing field. The play area can be either square or rectangular. At a signal (e.g., a whistle), each team attempts to move as quickly as possible to the corner directly across (diagonally) from its own. While moving across the open space, team members must perform or accomplish given tasks (run, hop, skip, crab walk, walk backwards, wheelbarrow race, or piggyback). The first team to get all its members into a new corner wins that particular round. It is suggested that the first round be fairly simple and that safety be stressed. This is especially true for where the teams must cross paths in the middle of the room. There will be mass bedlam in the center whenever all four teams crisscross. Safety Guards should be posted and ready for action.

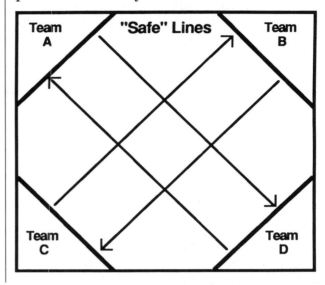

Bomb Drill

Good for play either indoors or outdoors, this is a very active game that tends to tire kids out. Before the game can begin, Safety Guards must be designated and the group must select names for the two opposite walls in the room or sides of the playing field. Players start in a huddle in the middle of the room or field. The leader then calls out the name of one of the sides and the group must run like crazy to that side. The leader continues to call out the names of the sides to indicate which side the group is to go to. While the group is running between these points, the leader may call out one of the following three instructions:

FREEZE! Players must freeze right where they are.

BOMBS! Players must bend over, grab their knees, and keep their heads down.

TORPEDO! Players must dive to the floor in a push-up position. When any of these instructions is called, those designated as Safety Guards watch and call out of play the last person(s) to get into position. Players who get into the wrong position altogether are automatically out. The game continues with new instructions until only one person is left.

Crack the Whip

A favorite for years, this is an active, aggressive game that your group members have probably already played at school. It is also a game where safety is paramount. Clearly identify your Safety Guards and try to have them head off any potential problems. The game must be played outside in an area free of debris and ground holes. Play begins with players holding hands, creating a chain or whip of people. The designated leader of the line then begins to run, pulling the group along in a chain. The leader periodically changes directions, whipping the chain from one side to the other. Leaders should be changed frequently so that everyone gets a chance at "cracking the whip."

Domino

Good for large groups, this activity works best with multiple teams of twenty-five or more. All of the teams need to be exactly the same size. Each team forms a line parallel to the other teams with everyone facing in the same direction. At the whistle, the first person in each line squats, the next person in line follows suit, then the next person, and so on all the way down the line. Players cannot squat until the person immediately in front of them squats.

When the last person in line squats, he or she then quickly stands back up again, and the whole process repeats itself in reverse. Each person stands up in succession. Again, players cannot stand up until the person behind them has stood. The first team to complete the process backward and forward, is the winner.

The effect of this game visually is much like standing dominoes up side by side and pushing over the one on the end so that it knocks into the others. Each domino falls in succession to the end of the line. In this case the dominoes first go down, but then come back up again. The game can be repeated with encouragement to step up the pace. Safety Guards are a good idea for this activity.

Drop the Keys

After appointing a Safety Guard, select a safe area for play that has clear boundaries and can accommodate players sitting in chairs that have been scattered throughout the room. One person is designated as "It." This person is without a chair but is given a set of keys to carry. The objective is to get a chair in the course of play. The game begins as "It" walks quickly among the chairs and grabs the hand of one of the players seated in a chair. The person whose hand is grabbed then takes hold of someone else's hand. The process continues as those holding hands keep walking quickly throughout the scattered chairs. As the line gets longer, "It" goes under arms and between people to thoroughly tie the line in knots. All the while, the person at the other end of the line is attempting to grab on to another player sitting in a chair. At any given point "It" can drop the set of keys. This signals all those holding hands to make a mad dash for an empty chair. The player left without a chair becomes the next "It."

Dr. Tangle

This game requires close contact and cooperation among the group members. If a group is not comfortable with close physical contact between boys and girls, single sex groupings are advised. First, appoint a Safety Guard. Then organize players in groups of six to twenty, making sure the total number in any one group is an even number. Instruct each group to form a tight circle facing inward. Then have everyone extend their right hands into the circle and take hold of someone else's right hand (though not the hands of those on their immediate right or left). Once right hands are joined, have participants extend their left hands into the circle and take someone else's left hand (again avoiding the hands of those to their immediate right and left).

Now without letting go of hands, the group must maneuver into one large circle by twisting, turning, and going under and over each other. The task can be done but it requires a coordinated effort on the part of the group members.

For added fun have someone be "Dr. Tangle." This person's job is to try to untangle the group without breaking their grips. Dr. Tangle gives directions to the group as to how they are to untangle themselves. Dr. Tangle can do surgery one time (break grips of one couple) in an attempt to get the group untangled. When there is more than one group, teams can compete to see which group can disentangle itself first.

Earthquake

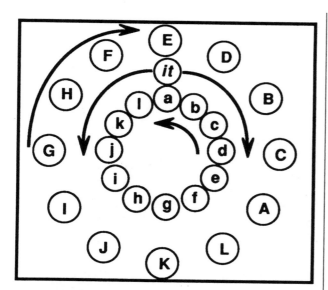

Select one person to be "It" and organize the remaining players into two concentric circles of the same size. The outer circle should face inward and the inner circle should face outward. Each player from the inner circle will then have a partner in the outer circle. Space the circles so that "It" can walk between the inner and the outer partners. When given a signal the outer circle moves clockwise, while the inner circle moves counterclockwise. "It" walks in between the two circles in either direction. Once the circles are moving, "It" calls out "Earthquake!" and stomps both feet on the ground. The players in the outer and inner circles must then hurry to find their partners. This action will recreate the two concentric circles except that "It" can connect with any player in the outer circle, thus leaving one player without a partner. This player becomes the new "It" and the game begins again. The game can also be played with more than one "It."

Fruitbasket Upset

Usually played inside, this game can involve any number of people. Whatever the size, the entire group sits in a circle with one less chair than there are people. The extra person stands in the middle as "It." Everyone is assigned the name of a fruit. With large groups you can have several people identified with the same category of fruit. Generally it is best to avoid having too many different categories so that all the players can get a chance to play.

The game begins with "It" calling out the names of one or more fruits. The people who are assigned those fruits must exchange chairs. During the exchange, "It" tries to claim one of the vacated chairs. The person who fails to get a chair becomes the new "It." The player who is "It" also has the option of calling out "Fruitbasket Upset," at which time everyone must exchange chairs. Be sure to use sturdy chairs as this game is really wild. People often end up in each other's laps or on the floor. Safety Guards should be appointed and ready to intervene when necessary. The game can also be played outdoors using small circles mapped out with tape on the ground. Safety Guards can make calls over disputes about who reached a circle first.

Hula Hoop Pack

Divide into teams of equal size. Each team tries to see how many kids they can get inside a hula hoop. If a genuine hula hoop is not available, then any strong hoop or a thick rope tied into a circle also will work. If your kids enjoy this quickie mixer, try packing them into other things like tractor tires or any other safe object.

I Like Everyone

Similar to "Fruitbasket Upset" and other games where people scramble for chairs, players begin by positioning their chairs in a circle with plenty of space between each chair. Only one person is without a chair and that person is "It." This person stands in the middle of the circle and says, "I like everyone except . . . " and names a characteristic of at least two people in the group. For example, "It" might say, "I like everyone, except those wearing shoes!" or "I like everyone, except those with blonde hair!" Players with the characteristic named must then vacate their chairs and scramble to find new ones. "It" also seeks to get a chair and whoever is caught standing without a chair at the end becomes the new "It."

Only those people in the chairs who have that characteristic have to vacate their chairs. Everyone else can sit still. Those who vacate their chairs must find new ones, but they cannot stand up and then sit back down in the same chair. The person in the middle, however, may say, "I like everyone," in which case *everyone* must get up and scramble to find a new chair. This creates quite a traffic jam!

Jericho and Jerusalem

Select one person to be "It" and have the other players stand in a circle. The player who is "It" stands in the middle of the circle and chooses an action or gesture, such as squatting, jumping up and down, or saluting. The game begins when "It" calls out either "Jericho" or "Jerusalem." At the call "Jerusalem," players must imitate the action or gesture selected by "It." The call of "Jericho" requires the players to stand still. "It" can seek to confuse the group by stretching out the word, saying "Jeeeeeeerrrrricho" or "Jeeeeeeerrrrrusalem." The last player to follow the instructions, or the one who makes an incorrect response, gets to be the new "It."

Knock Your Socks Off

Mark out a big circle on the floor using either tape or chalk. Have players remove their shoes, leaving their socks on. All players then get into the circle and at the command "Go," they all seek to take other players' socks off while keeping their own on. When a player's socks have both been pulled off, the player is out of the game. A player is also out of the game when any part of his or her body moves outside of the circle. The last player to keep on at least one sock is the winner. Appoint Safety Guards for this one, as the group can get rather wild.

Line Pull

After appointing a Safety Guard, divide the group into two teams of equal size. Position the teams facing each other on opposite sides of a line marked on the floor. The object of the game is for each team to try to increase its numbers by pulling players from the other team over the line to its side. Players must stay within three feet of the line at all times. At the command "Go," players from Team A try to pull Team B's players over to Team A's side of the line and vice

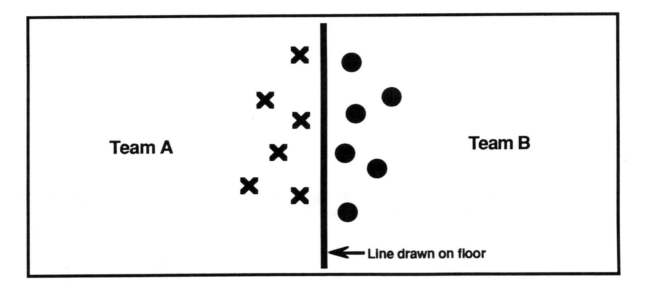

versa. Players must try to reach out and grab someone on the other side without stepping over the line. Players that go over the line automatically become members of the opposing team. At the command "Stop!" the players must freeze and the winning team is then determined.

Musical Backs

A variation on "Musical Chairs," this game begins with players simply wandering around the room. When the music stops or when the whistle blows, everyone quickly finds another person and stands back-to-back. When there is an odd number of people on the floor, someone will end up without a partner. This person is now out of the game. When there is an even number of people on the floor, a chair is placed in the middle. Anyone may sit in the chair and be safe, thus leaving an odd number of people to find partners with which to stand back-to-back. Players must keep moving and may not pair off with the same person twice in a row. Play continues until there is only one pair remaining.

Nerds Do This

Another variation of "Simon Says," this game begins with the players standing in a circle facing inward. One person is selected to be "It" and stands in the center of the circle. "It" models an action or gesture while saying, "Nerds do this." All the players in the circle must then imitate the action or gesture performed. Play continues with different actions and gestures as "It" continues inviting the group to follow by saying, "Nerds do this." At some point "It" performs an action prefaced only by, "Do this." Any player caught copying this action must drop out of play. The game continues until everyone has been eliminated. The caught player can also become "It."

Poop Deck

This game works well with as few as ten players or as many as 100. Play requires a fairly large room or an open space outside. The play area is marked off into three sections using either tape or chalk. One section is the "Poop Deck," one is the "Main Deck," and one is the "Quarter Deck." A leader calls out the name of a deck and the players must run to that deck or section. The last person into the section is out. The leader may call the name of any section, even the name of the one where the group is currently standing. If kids are in the "Poop Deck" section and the leader calls that section, anyone who crosses the line or jumps the gun is out. This format continues at a rapid pace until one person is the winner.

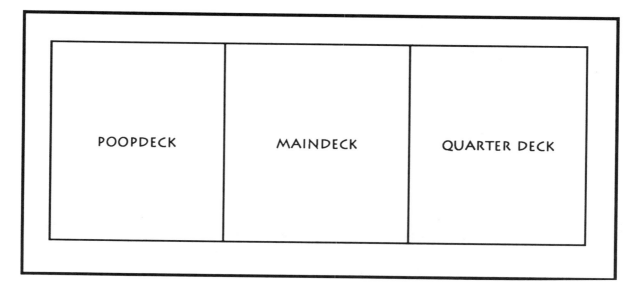

It is suggested that players be given a few trial runs to warm up and get a feel for the game. Leaders should also take care to make their calls loud and distinct to avoid confusion.

The basic format of the game can be

varied by adding additional decks and/or interspersing alternate commands. Some possibilities are noted below.

Additional Decks:

Second Deck	Bridge Deck
Third Deck	Flight Deck
Fourth Deck	Hanger Deck
Promenade Deck	Upper Deck
Boat Deck	Forecastle Deck
Sun Deck	Cabin Deck

Alternate Commands:

HIT THE DECK! Players drop to a prone position.

CLEAR THE DECK! Players step completely outside the marked area and may not step back in until they hear the command, ON DECK!

ON DECK! Players are free to step back inside the marked area.

Pull Off

Easy to play, this is a wild game that older children really enjoy. It can get rough, so appoint Safety Guards to monitor the game closely. The game begins with all of the boys huddled together inside a circle with their arms locked. Their goal is to remain inside the circle. The goal of the girls is to pull boys outside of the circle. Girls can be as resourceful as they wish, but should be cautioned not to injure anyone with their fingernails. Boys are limited to using their physical strength in hanging together.

Red Light! Green Light!

A classic among childhood games, this may well be one you remember from your own past. The game can be played with as few as five players, but it can be played with many more. One player is selected to be "It" and stands fifteen to twenty-five feet away from the other players. The other players start behind a line that has been marked on the ground using either chalk or tape. "It" stands facing away from the group and calls out "Green Light!" to signal the players to move. A call of "Red Light!" signals the players to stop and freeze in their tracks. After calling "Red Light!" "It" turns around as quickly as possible to try and catch players that are still in motion. Those caught are sent back to the starting line. "It" again faces away from the group to issue the "Green Light!" signal. The objective for the players is to be the first one to touch "It" and take over as the new "It."

Red Light! Green Light! In the Round

This game is played just like "Red Light! Green Light!" except that players stand in a large circle. Mark the circle's boundaries with chalk or tape. "It" stands in the center of the circle and players stand at the circle's edge. "It" closes her or his eyes when calling out "Green Light!" or "Red Light!" Anyone caught moving must return to the outer perimeter of the circle.

Sardines

This game is similar to "Hide and Seek." It requires a large area with lots of good hiding places. The group chooses one person to be "It." This person hides while the rest of the group counts to 100, or until a signal is given. The group then sets out to find the hidden "It." Each player should look individually, but small groups of two or three may look together. Players who find "It" join in the hiding, trying to remain hidden from the rest of the group. Those hiding may even change the hiding place during the course of the game. The last person to find the hidden group of players, which has surely by now come to resemble a can of sardines, becomes "It" for the next game.

Easy-to-Do Meeting Starters

Here you will find a wide variety of fun, creatively entertaining, and engaging crowd breakers that are certain to grab your kids' attention.

Artist's Imagination

Divide the group into teams, supplying each team with a pencil and several pieces of paper. Position the teams around the room and station a leader in the middle. Ask a representative from each team to go to the leader who will quietly whisper the name of an item that the representatives must draw for their teams. At a signal, the representatives return to their teams and begin to draw. They cannot speak or make any sounds, and they are not allowed to write any words on their drawings. Team members try to guess what their "artist" is drawing. The first team to shout out the correct answer wins. Possible items to sketch include:

A pizza	A paper clip
Sunday school teacher	A mirror
A tube of toothpaste	A telephone
Banana split	The Three Bears

The team artists can also be asked to depict Bible stories through their drawings. This adds another dimension to the game and increases the level of difficulty. Listed below are Bible stories that work well.

The Flood	Christ's Second Coming
The Woman at the Well	The Last Supper
Daniel in the Lion's Den	The Good Samaritan
Jonah and the Whale	David and Goliath
Cain and Abel	Sermon on the Mount

Bible Character Guess

This game is set up like a TV talk show, with volunteers acting out the parts of Bible characters. Audience teams try to guess who the characters are. Participants are first divided into teams of three. One or more teams then volunteer to leave the room to select a Bible character or characters to portray. When depicting more than one character, the characters are to be related in some way. For example, they might choose Samson and Delilah, Noah and his three sons, or Paul and Timothy. The volunteers return to the room, taking positions "on stage" before the audience teams. Their job is to assume the roles of the biblical character(s), talking to each other as if they were guests on a TV talk show. The object of the game is for the audience teams to guess who the characters are. The audience may ask questions of the volunteers about the roles they are portraying, but each team is given a limited number of guesses as to the identities of the Bible characters. Teams can rotate asking questions until one team correctly identifies the character(s).

The Contagious Game

Position group members in a circle so that everyone can see each other. One person sets things in motion by voicing an "ailment." For example, he or she might say: "My right eye twitches." All members in the group must then start twitching their right eyes. A second person voices another "ailment," saying perhaps: "My left foot has the jumps," or "I have whooping cough." Everyone must then follow suit, adding the second ailment to the first. After a few people share their ailments, everyone should be jumping, twitching, coughing, sneezing, and generally having a great time. This is a prime opportunity for videotaping; it is sure to provide lots of laughs when played back for the group.

Hmmm... An interesting outbreak of Jumping Left Foot Syndrome.

Dark Draw

Everyone in the group is given a sheet of paper along with a pen or marker. With all the lights out, participants are given five minutes to draw anything they want. Pictures are then judged, with everyone winning some sort of prize. Awards can be given for the silliest, craziest, best, and worst.

Fingers-Up Playoffs

A good test for quick thinking, this game involves a series of one-to-one "playoffs." After dividing the group into pairs, have partners face one another with their hands behind their backs. At the count of three, they hold up both hands in front of their faces, holding up a number of fingers on each hand. A closed fist means zero on that hand. The first partner to voice the total number of fingers held up on all four hands wins the round. Each pair should go for the best of two out of three.

Winners from each pair are then matched up for additional playoffs until it winds down to a championship match between two people. Give the winner a prize that can be shared with everyone, like finger foods.

First-Guess Favorite

How well do your kids *really* know each other? Hand out a copy of the next page to each member of your group and find out! This one works great for larger groups of kids.

First Name Answers

This is a simple but fun name game. The leader asks various group members a question that they must answer with a single word. The word must begin with the first letter of their first names. If asked the question, "What makes you laugh?" someone named Kathy might say, "Kangaroos" or someone named Todd might say, "Toads." The game can be made more difficult by requiring two-word responses. Players must then respond to questions with one word beginning with the initial for their first names and a second word beginning with the initial for their last names. If asked, "What do you like to do after school?" someone named Jason Nichols might answer, "Just Nothing." A Dianna Wilson might say, "Doing Work." Answers will range from the hilarious to the ridiculous. Below are some questions that could be asked.

1. What are you afraid of?
2. What makes you cry?
3. If you had $1,000, what would you do?

First-Guess Favorite

Directions:
First, put a check to the left of your own favorites in each category. Then move around the room and guess what the favorites are of others in the group. If you guess correctly on the first try, have that person put her or his initials to the right of the appropriate category on your sheet. You may get no more than two initials from the same person.

1. **Favorite Music** _____
   - ☐ Country and western
   - ☐ Classical
   - ☐ Rock and roll
   - ☐ Contemporary Christian

2. **Favorite Food** _____
   - ☐ Mexican
   - ☐ American (meat and potatoes)
   - ☐ Chinese
   - ☐ Italian

3. **Favorite Movies** _____
   - ☐ Adventure
   - ☐ Comedy
   - ☐ Mystery
   - ☐ Science fiction

4. **Favorite Car** _____
   - ☐ Luxury
   - ☐ Sports
   - ☐ Economy
   - ☐ Truck

5. **Favorite Vacation** _____
   - ☐ Beach
   - ☐ Mountains
   - ☐ World travel
   - ☐ Sightseeing America (by car)

6. **Favorite Sweet** _____
   - ☐ Pie
   - ☐ Cake
   - ☐ Ice cream
   - ☐ Candy

7. **Favorite Animal** _____
   - ☐ Dog
   - ☐ Cat
   - ☐ Bird
   - ☐ Fish

8. **Favorite TV Show** _____
   - ☐ News program
   - ☐ Comedy
   - ☐ Drama
   - ☐ Cartoons

9. **Favorite Sport** _____
   - ☐ Football
   - ☐ Basketball
   - ☐ Baseball/Softball
   - ☐ Soccer

10. **Favorite Reading Material** _____
    - ☐ Comic books
    - ☐ Magazines
    - ☐ Newspapers
    - ☐ Books

11. **Favorite Color** _____
    - ☐ Dark (black, brown, rust)
    - ☐ Light (white, gray, tan)
    - ☐ Pastel (yellow, pink, baby blue)
    - ☐ Bright (red, orange, blue)

12. **Favorite Season** _____
    - ☐ Winter
    - ☐ Spring
    - ☐ Summer
    - ☐ Fall

13. **Favorite Time of Day** _____
    - ☐ Early morning
    - ☐ Afternoon
    - ☐ Evening
    - ☐ Late night

4. What is the thing you look forward to the most about being a teenager?
5. If you could miss school for one week, what would you do?
6. What things bother your parents the most?
7. What do you like most about school?
8. How do you want to spend this weekend?
9. What would be fun for our group to do at summer camp?
10. What do you like for lunch?

Geiger Counter

A good group energizer, this activity requires a volunteer to leave the room for a few minutes. While this person is away, the rest of the group selects a very ordinary object (chalkboard, eraser, paper clip, pencil, or Sunday school quarterly) and agrees on a hiding place. The leader then hides the object. The volunteer is then asked to return. She or he must try to find the object, not knowing what it is. Everyone else is seated and together they serve as a type of Geiger counter, "tick-tick-ticking" slowly as the volunteer moves away from the object and faster as the volunteer approaches the object. This continues until the hidden object is found. New volunteers can be selected for additional rounds of play.

Gorilla-Person-Gun

This game is a lot like the old "Paper-Rock-Scissors" game children play. Players stand in two lines, pairing off with the person across from them. Partners then stand with their backs to each other. A leader directs the activity by counting out loud, "One, two, three!" On three, players turn to face their partners and immediately assume one of three positions:
1. **Gorilla**—hands up in the air, teeth snarling, and shouting loudly, "Grrrooowwwlll."
2. **Person**—hands on hips saying, "Hi, there."
3. **Gun**—both hands draw imaginary guns from hips and shoot, shouting, "Bang!"

There can be no hesitation in deciding which position to take. Once the turn is complete, each pair must determine a winner using the following guidelines.
1. "Person" versus "Gun" results in the "Person" winning because the "Person" has power over the "Gun."
2. "Gun" versus "Gorilla" results in the "Gun" winning because the "Gorilla" can be shot by the "Gun."
3. "Gorilla" versus "Person" results in the "Gorilla" winning because the "Gorilla" can kill a "Person."
4. If both partners assume the same position, they both win and try again. Should they tie a second time, they both lose.

After the first round, the losers are eliminated from play. The winners pair up again to play a second round. With each round some players are eliminated. Rounds continue until there is only one pair remaining. They play a final round to decide the winner.

Hand over Hand

Divide your group into two or more teams, each with at least five participants. Each team forms a circle. Players hold their right hands into the middle of the circle, stacking them together, "basketball huddle style." Once their right hands are in position, players stack their left hands on top of the right hand stack. Then, at a signal, the person whose hand is on the bottom should take that hand and place it on top of the stack. The next person should do the same, and so on, until the person who began the process is again on the bottom. The first team to complete the process is the winner of the round. The next round, try three "laps." Then try five. After everyone is getting the hang of it, try going backward.

I Like My Church

Write out on slips of paper, "I like my church because _____ ." Have the group sit in a circle and distribute the slips, along with pencils, to each person. Instruct them to write a single phrase completing the statement. When the

> *I like my Church because my friends are there.*
>
> *And the pastor wears pink polka-dotted underwear.*

kids have written their phrases, have them pass their slips to the person on the right. Now instruct that person to write another sentence or phrase that will rhyme with the first. Then collect them and read them out loud.

Leader Shuffle

A positive first experience with new leaders can set the pace for future relationships in a group of young kids. This activity provides an excellent non-threatening approach to letting kids see the human side of their new leaders.

Begin by dividing the group into as many small groups as there are new leaders. Give each small group three minutes to compile a list of questions that they want to ask the new leader(s). Possible questions could be: "How old are you?" "Are you married?" "Do you have kids?" or "What was fifth grade like for you?" Once the groups have identified some questions, assign one new leader to each group. The group should introduce themselves to the leader. They can then have three to five minutes (or more, if you wish) to ask their questions. When the time is up, the leaders rotate to another group. This continues until every group has had an opportunity to meet with each new leader.

Let's Get Acquainted

Here's a meeting starter that serves well to facilitate interaction in even the largest of groups. Distribute a photocopy of the following page to each member of the group. Have everyone fill in each blank on the page with the name of someone who fits the description. The first person to get all the blanks filled, or the one who has the most at the end of the time limit, is the winner. You can also be creative and come up with a list of your own, or try letting your kids do so.

Let's Get Acquainted

1. Find someone who was not born in this town _____ .

2. Find someone who does well in arithmetic _____ .

3. Find someone who is on a soccer team _____ .

4. Find someone who plays a musical instrument _____ .

5. Find someone who uses your brand of toothpaste _____ .

6. Find someone who watches cartoons on Saturday mornings _____ .

7. Find someone who is not allowed to watch MTV _____ .

8. Find someone who likes his or her brother or sister _____ .

9. Find someone who does not know your last name _____ .

Marvelous Matthew

Introductions need not be boring. With group members sitting in a circle, ask them each to think of a positive adjective that begins with the first letter of their name (Jock Jason, Kind Kevin, Super Stephanie, Awesome Alisha, Brainy Bob, and so on). Starting anywhere around the circle have someone begin the introductions, stating their first name along with the positive adjective. The person on the right then repeats the first person's name (including the adjective) and states his or her own name in the same way. The game continues around the circle with each group member having to repeat the names of everyone who has gone before them. This means that the last person gets to name everyone. Listed below are some suggestions to help ensure success with this activity.

- If you have a large group, break into smaller groups of ten to fifteen.
- Give kids and adult leaders time at the beginning of the activity to think of the positive adjective that describes them.
- Group members not able to come up with an adjective are allowed to ask the group for help.
- Younger kids might name something they like to eat or do instead of an adjective, and it does not have to begin with the first letter of their names. For example: "My name is Amy and I like pizza."

Name That Person

Here's a good competitive game that helps kids get to know each other better. Depending on the size of the group, divide into two or four teams of equal size. If working with four teams, then work toward a playoff between the two winning teams and the two losing teams from the first round.

Before the game begins, give all players a blank three-by-five card (or piece of paper) and have them write down five little-known, true facts about themselves and then sign their names. For example:

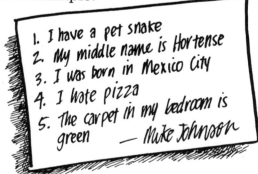

1. I have a pet snake
2. My middle name is Hortense
3. I was born in Mexico City
4. I hate pizza
5. The carpet in my bedroom is green — Mike Johnson

Collect all the cards and keep separate stacks for each team. The game is now ready to be played. Each team's objective is to name the person on their cards using as few clues as possible. Play begins with each team bidding for a chance to guess a person's name. Bidding involves the number of clues: "We can name that person in five clues!" "We can name that person in four clues!" and so on. The team that wins the bidding gets to guess the top card of the opposite team. They then have five seconds to guess after receiving the appropriate number of clues. Teams can huddle together to come up with an answer, but appointing a spokesperson will help keep things orderly. The more interaction between the team members the better. If a team makes an incorrect guess or if they do not answer in five seconds, the points go to the other team.

The scoring goes like this:

1 clue   = 50 points
2 clues = 40 points
3 clues = 30 points
4 clues = 20 points
5 clues = 10 points

The game proceeds until every card has been guessed at at least once. After each card has been played, you can read the rest of the clues that are on it and if the original guess was wrong, you can let them try to guess again. At the end, the team with the most points wins.

People Machines

Divide up into groups of seven or eight. Each group has the task of becoming a machine, such as a washing machine, a tape recorder, or a VCR. Each individual must be a working part with a suitable sound. The machines are then presented to the rest of the group who must try to guess what machine is being portrayed.

Plausible Reasons

An opportunity for creative thinking, this game capitalizes on being a bit zany and wild. Have kids break into small groups of three or four. Provide each group with pencils and paper and assign them the task of coming up with the most *outrageous* answers to three questions. Some sample questions are listed below.

1. Explain why so many people believe in the existence of the large, hairy, humanlike creature known as the Abominable Snowman.
2. Describe how airplanes stay in the air.
3. Give your reason for the disappearance of the Garden of Eden.
4. Explain why people get hiccups.
5. Give your explanation for the phases of the moon.
6. Describe what life on another planet might look like.
7. Explain why teenagers act the way they do.
8. Tell where the white goes when snow melts.
9. Explain why some people have belly buttons that are "innies," and others have "outies."
10. Tell why "i" comes before "e" except after "c."
11. Explain how zebras got their stripes.
12. Tell how long your toenails would grow if you never trimmed them.
13. Explain why kids get grown-up teeth.
14. Describe how the world would be different if kids were in charge.
15. Explain why foods that are good for you taste so bad.

Kids will have fun creating answers as well as listening to the answers made up by the other groups.

This activity is ideal when you have a group of kids who know each other fairly well, but who, as a group, could use some positive affirmation.

Positive People Bingo

Directions: Find people who fit the descriptions in the boxes below. Ask each person you find to sign their first name in the square that you believe describes them. The winner is the first person to get all the squares filled with signatures. The same person can sign only once.

Is very friendly _____	Really talented _____	Likes sports _____
Cares about others _____	Has helped me before _____	Has a good sense of humor _____
Is easy to talk to _____	Is a fun person _____	Has a nice smile _____

Shoe Grab Relay

This relay game is suitable for large group get-togethers (the bigger the group, the better). To start, everyone needs to take off his and her shoes and put them in a big pile at one end of the room. As kids this age can be sensitive about foot odor, adults will need to be excited about doing this. The shoes are then mixed up as much as possible. Then, divide the group into even teams for the relay.

At a signal, the first person in each team must turn to the next person in line and describe her or his shoes to them. That person must then run to the pile and hunt out the shoes described, bring them back, and put them on the person. If they are the wrong shoes, they must go back again and get the right ones. The game continues in this manner with the last person in line describing her or his shoes to the first person in line. The team who has all its shoes on first is the winning team. The game is especially fun when lots of the kids wear similar shoes; it can make it almost impossible to find the right shoes.

Shoe Scramble

Here again, everyone removes her or his own shoes and places them in one big pile. Everyone then gathers around the pile of shoes at some set distance. At a signal all the players run to the pile and choose two different shoes, neither of which should belong to them. Putting these shoes on, without tying them, the players then begin the search for their own shoes. To do so they must first find the matches to the shoes they are wearing. When a player finds a matching shoe, he or she puts the shoe next to the match and the two players then walk, shoe-to-shoe, around the group looking for the matches to their other shoes. The group will quickly become a tangled mess.

The Sit Down Game

Here's a good meeting starter to use with both parents and kids. Ask everyone to stand up; announce that you will be reading a list of "If" characteristics. When the "If" characteristic applies to them, people are to sit down. For example, you might say, "Sit down if you are getting a bad grade in spelling." Each person must decide if the description fits. Once a player sits down, he or she must remain seated. The fun to the game is in how creative you are in coming up with "If" characteristics. Here are a few examples of good ones, but it's usually best if you add some original ones that fit your particular group.

Sit Down . . .
- If you have worn the same socks for two days.
- If you like spinach.
- If you still believe in Santa Claus.
- If your mother dresses you.
- If you pick your nose.

- If you pick other people's noses.
- If your nose is running.
- If you wear "Underoos."
- If you are really good-looking.
- Stand up if the person next to you just sat down and was wrong!
- If you have a hole in your sock.
- If you still suck your thumb.

- If you read comic books.
- If you wake up early for Saturday morning cartoons.
- If you watch "Sesame Street."

End with, "Sit down if you are tired of standing," and that will usually get everyone down.

Spontaneous Poetry

Break into small groups of seven to ten and provide each group with a pencil and a piece of paper. The first person in the group writes down a word at the top of the piece of paper and passes it to the next person. The second person contemplates the first word and writes another word just below the first one. Then, folding the paper so the first word cannot be seen, the paper is passed to a third person who looks at the second word and writes down a third.

This process is repeated until everyone in the group has contributed a word. Group members can write down any kind of word (provided it is decent), but they should not spend a lot of time thinking about the "right" word. When the last word has been written down, the paper can be unfolded and the "poem" can be

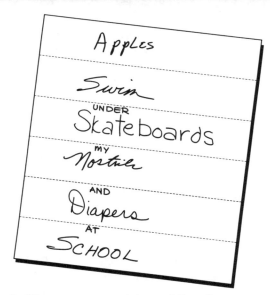

read. You may want to add a few connecting words, like verbs or prepositions, to make the "poem" read more smoothly.

Stack 'Em Up

Prepare in advance a list of qualifying characteristics like those found in the examples below.

1. If you forgot to use a deodorant today . . .
2. If you have a hole in your sock . . .
3. If you are afraid of the dark . . .
4. If you have brown (or blonde or red or black) hair . . .
5. If you took a bath last night . . .
6. If you have an older (or younger) brother . . .
7. If you have a younger (or older) sister . . .
8. If you are an only child . . .
9. If you live in an apartment (or house or mobile home or town house) . . .
10. If you live north of here (or south or

18. If you passed your last arithmetic test . . .
19. If you are in the school band . . .
20. If you are over five feet, two inches tall (or under five feet, two inches tall) . . .
21. If you are wearing a watch . . .
22. If you play an after-school sport . . .
23. If you missed a day of school in the last week . . .
24. If you wear braces . . .
25. If you wear glasses . . .
26. If you are in the school chorus . . .
27. If you have memorized a Scripture verse in the last week . . .
28. If you are cool . . .
29. If you are wearing a belt . . .
30. If you brought a Bible with you . . . .

Have everyone sit in chairs in a circle. Read the qualifying characteristics one at a time, adding particular instructions each time. Instructions might be to " . . . move three chairs to the right" or " . . . move one chair to the left," and so on. In other words, if you were to say, "If you forgot to use a deodorant today, move two chairs to the right," all those who qualify must move as instructed and sit in that chair, even if it is already occupied. As the game progresses, kids begin "stacking up" on certain chairs.

east or west) . . .
11. If you visited your grandparents in the last week . . .
12. If you have to baby-sit your little brother (or sister) . . .
13. If you are wearing colored underwear . . .
14. If you received an "A" on your last spelling test . . .
15. If you have blue eyes (or brown or green or hazel or gray or violet) . . .
16. If you watched TV last night . . .
17. If you have watched MTV when your parents did not know about it . . .

Taking a Trip

Here is one meeting starter that is certain to tax everyone's concentration. The leader starts by saying, "I'm taking a trip and I'm bringing _____ ." He or she can bring anything as long as it is only one word. The second person repeats the sentence and adds one item to the list. The third person adds another, and the game continues as long as the list is repeated correctly in order. If a person forgets an item or gets them out of order, he or she is eliminated or the game can begin again.

Why and Because

Give everyone in the group a pencil and two three-by-five cards. Have each person write out a question on one card beginning with the word "Why." Collect these. Now have everyone write out answers on cards that begin with "Because." Collect these cards as well and then randomly redistribute both sets. Have kids read the questions they received along with the answers.

A fun variation is a game called "Problems and Solutions." It is played the same way, except on one card players write a problem and on another card they write a solution (unrelated to the problem they wrote). The results are things like:

Problem: "What do I do when I have too much homework?"

Solution: "Ask for more lunch money!"

Zigzag

Pass out paper and pencils to everyone. Ask each person to draw three lines. They can be straight or zigzag. Then have everyone exchange papers and ask the new owners of the papers to draw a picture using the already drawn three lines as starting points. You can hang the pictures up for all to admire.

Emergency Teaching Activities

These minimum-preparation teaching activities are ideal for on-the-spot lessons or discussions.

Grab-Bag Testimonies from the Psalms

This idea provides an opportunity for your kids to reflect on their present spiritual condition and to share their thoughts with others. Select and photocopy a number of the "Grab-bag Testimony" cards found on the following three pages. Each of the cards contains a passage of Scripture and a sentence instructing the participants to read the Scripture and relate the passage to their lives.

During your meeting time, ask volunteers to reach into a paper bag and take out one of the "Testimony" cards. Give them time to look over the cards and to collect their thoughts. Then ask those with cards to share, one at a time. (Be careful to give these volunteers the option of not participating if they feel too "on the spot.") You should be prepared to ask one or two follow-up questions of each person to help each respond in a personal way. The activity doesn't take a lot of time, but it can help to create a sense of community within your group.

"Blessed is the man who does not walk in the counsel of the wicked or stand in the way of sinners or sit in the seat of mockers." Psalm 1:1

———

Read this passage out loud and tell the group why the Bible warns us here to choose the right kind of friends.

"The Lord is my rock, my fortress, and my deliverer; my God is my rock, in whom I take refuge. He is my shield and the horn of my salvation, my stronghold." Psalm 18:2

———

Explain to the group, after reading the passage out loud, why the Lord is like a fort where one can go for safety!

"But let all who take refuge in you be glad; let them ever sing for joy. Spread your protection over them, that those who love your name may rejoice in you. For surely, O Lord, you bless the righteous; you surround them with your favor as with a shield." Psalm 5:11-12

———

Read this verse to the group and tell how you feel God has protected you!

"The heavens declare the glory of God; the skies proclaim the work of his hands. Day after day they pour forth speech; night after night they display knowledge." Psalm 19:1-2

———

Read the passage to the group and then describe how God's creation tells us about him!

"I will praise you, O Lord, with all my heart; I will tell of all your wonders. I will be glad and rejoice in you; I will sing praise to your name, O Most High." Psalm 9:1-2

———

Read this passage to the group and tell two reasons why you want to praise the Lord!

"The Lord is my shepherd, I shall not be in want. He makes me lie down in green pastures, he leads me beside quiet waters, he restores my soul. He guides me in paths of righteousness for his name's sake." Psalm 23:1-3

———

Read the passage to the group. Then tell how the Lord is your shepherd!

"I have set the Lord always before me. Because he is at my right hand, I will not be shaken." Psalm 16:8

———

After reading this verse, share with the group members how they can think more about the Lord and involve him more in their lives.

"Remember not the sins of my youth and my rebellious ways; according to your love remember me, for you are good, O Lord." Psalm 25:7

———

Tell the group, after reading the passage, why all of us as Christians can be thankful for this verse!

"Whoever of you loves life and desires to see many good days, keep your tongue from evil and your lips from speaking lies." Psalm 34:12-13

———

Read this passage of Scripture to the group members and explain to them why you feel we are warned in the Bible to carefully watch what we say.

"Be still, and know that I am God; I will be exalted among the nations, I will be exalted in the earth." Psalm 46:10

———

Tell the group, after reading this verse, about a time when it was quiet and peaceful and you honored God in the silence.

"Do not fret because of evil men or be envious of those who do wrong; for like the grass they will soon wither, like green plants they will soon die away." Psalm 37:1-2

———

Read these verses to the group and tell how you have or have not put this into practice in your life.

"For this God is our God for ever and ever; he will be our guide even to the end." Psalm 48:14

———

Read this verse and share with the group how God is your God and how he has guided you!

"O Lord, do not forsake me; be not far from me, O my God. Come quickly to help me, O Lord my Savior." Psalm 38:21-22

———

Read this passage to the group and then talk about why you need the Lord to be close to you!

"Have mercy on me, O God, according to your unfailing love; according to your great compassion blot out my transgressions. Wash away all my iniquity and cleanse me from my sin." Psalm 51:1-2

———

Read this passage to the group. Then explain why you need to confess your sins to God!

"God is our refuge and strength, an ever-present help in trouble. Therefore we will not fear, though the earth give way and the mountains fall into the heart of the sea, though its waters roar and foam and the mountains quake with their surging." Psalm 46:1-3

———

Read this passage and then describe to the group some of the things you fear, but that you would like to give to God.

"When I am afraid, I will trust in you. In God, whose word I praise, in God I trust; I will not be afraid. What can mortal man do to me?" Psalm 56:3-4

———

After reading this passage to the group, tell why you would want to trust in God when you are afraid!

"Say to God, 'How awesome are your deeds! So great is your power that your enemies cringe before you.' Come and see what God has done, how awesome his works in man's behalf!"
Psalm 66:3, 5

Read this passage to the group. Then describe some of the awesome works you have seen God do!

"Know that the Lord is God. It is he who made us, and we are his; we are his people, the sheep of his pasture."
Psalm 100:3

Describe for the group, after reading the verse out loud, how you live your life differently than people who do not believe God created them.

"For you have been my hope, O Sovereign Lord, my confidence since my youth. From birth I have relied on you; you brought me forth from my mother's womb. I will ever praise you."
Psalm 71:5-6

Read this out loud and then talk with the group about ways you have relied upon the Lord.

"Praise the Lord. Give thanks to the Lord, for he is good; his love endures forever." Psalm 106:1

Read the verse out loud and talk with the group about three things for which you are thankful.

"Hear my prayer, O Lord; listen to my cry for mercy. In the day of my trouble I will call to you, for you will answer me."
Psalm 86:6-7

Read these verses and talk with the group about a time God answered your prayers.

"You are good, and what you do is good; teach me your decrees."
Psalm 119:68

Read this verse to the group and tell one thing you feel you need to learn from God so that you can more closely follow him.

"Come, let us bow down in worship, let us kneel before the Lord our Maker; for he is our God and we are the people of his pasture, the flock under his care." Psalm 95:6-7

After reading this passage to the group, describe a time you felt especially close to God while in worship.

"For you created my inmost being; you knit me together in my mother's womb. I praise you because I am fearfully and wonderfully made; your works are wonderful, I know that full well." Psalm 139:13-14

After reading the passage, share with the group how it feels to know that God created you special.

My Life, Christ's Home

This activity is designed to help young people evaluate their commitment to Christ. Begin by reading and explaining Revelation 3:20. "Here I am! I stand at the door and knock. If anyone hears my voice and opens the door, I will come in and eat with him, and he with me."

Explain to the group that this passage of Scripture was written to the church in Laodicea during New Testament times. This particular church had proclaimed to know Christ but had really left him out of their church's day-to-day affairs. Christ was asking to be involved, to come back into their church. But Christ needed to be invited.

Discuss with the group members how we sometimes are like the church at Laodicea. We say we love Christ and want to follow him, but fail to reflect him in our lives. Ask them to imagine the whole of their lives as a big house with many rooms. Each room can serve to represent a different part of their lives. Jesus wants to be allowed into every room to make some changes—to redecorate, expand, or close off some parts—and to oversee the daily use of each room. Without total commitment, we may want to control certain rooms ourselves and shut Christ out of those rooms. Our goal is to examine our lives and to invite Christ into those areas we have kept to ourselves.

Give each young person in the group a copy of the "My Life, Christ's Home" worksheet found on the following page. Ask them to move with you through each room as you ask the following questions, or others that you wish to add. Then ask them to circle those rooms that need attention from Christ and list in those rooms the things they are willing to change.

Living Room
1. Are you choosing the right kinds of friends?
2. Do you tell others about Jesus?
3. Would your parents be proud of the choices you make?

Recreation Room
1. Are you making good choices in what you watch on television? At the movies?
2. Are the kinds of fun you have pleasing to God?

Family Room
1. Do you have fun with your family?
2. Do you spend enough time with your family?

Closet
1. Would the material things you own be pleasing to God?
2. Would Jesus say you had too many or not enough possessions?
3. Do you give some of what you have to God?

Kitchen
1. Are you eating healthy foods?
2. Are you doing your share of chores?
3. How do you help others in need (the hungry, the poor, the homeless)?

Dining Room
1. Do you practice good manners?
2. Are you kind to others?
3. Do you respect your parents? Your teachers?

Bathroom
1. Are you taking care of your body?
2. Are you preoccupied with your appearance?
3. Do you judge the way others look?

Bedroom
1. Are you spending time alone with God in prayer?
2. How often are you reading the Bible?
3. Are you getting enough sleep?
4. Are you doing your best in school and with your homework?

Summary Questions
1. Which rooms of your house are most occupied by Christ?
2. Which rooms are least occupied by Christ? (Which rooms did you circle?)
3. How does your "life/house" need to be remodeled?
4. What are some specific actions that you can take to make your house totally Christ's home?

MY LIFE, CHRIST'S HOME

Directions: As your leader guides you through each room,
circle the rooms that need attention from Christ and list in
each room what you are willing to change.

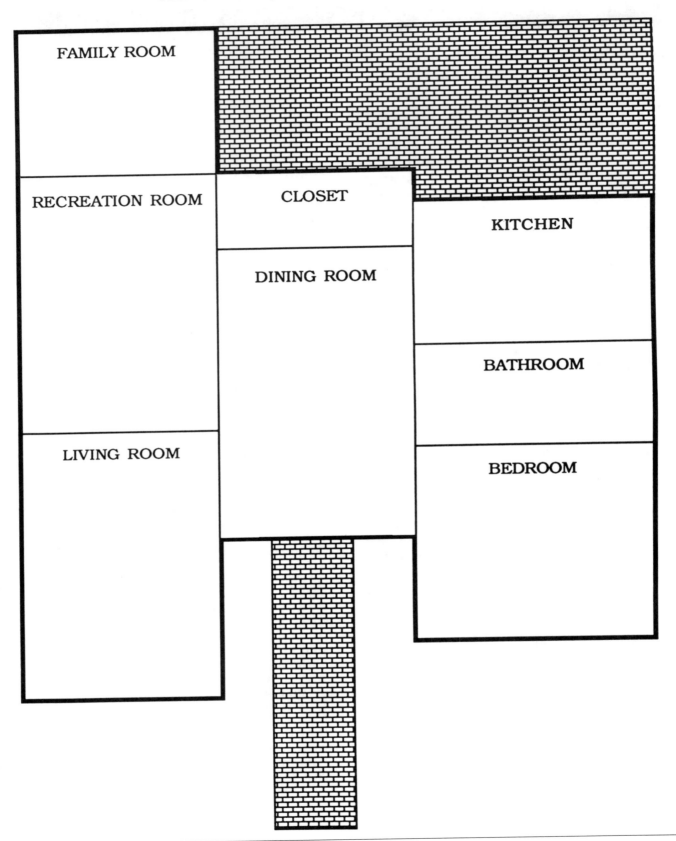

FAMILY ROOM

RECREATION ROOM

CLOSET

KITCHEN

DINING ROOM

BATHROOM

LIVING ROOM

BEDROOM

Picturing Forgiveness

Have your kids read the Bible passages listed on the worksheet on the following page. Then ask them to list as many word pictures as they can about how God forgives our sins. These word pictures might include throwing sins behind one's back, blotting out or wiping away sins, or erasing sins with a pencil eraser. Most kids ought to be able to come up with several pictures.

HE HAS REMOVED MY SIN AS FAR AS THE EAST IS FROM THE WEST — PSALM 103:11-12

After the kids have generated a list of word pictures, have them choose the one that seems to be most meaningful to them. Then give them some marking pens and paper, or other art supplies, and have them graphically depict their forgiveness word picture. When they are completed, allow each person to share the meaning of his or her picture with the rest of the group.

Finally, spend about five minutes with the entire group brainstorming a completely unique word picture for forgiveness, one not found in Scripture. You might want to make it very contemporary. This also can be graphically portrayed, perhaps as a large group mural to hang on the wall.

Prayerobics

Exercise is in! Help your kids to get in "prayer shape" by exercising thirty minutes to an hour in prayer. Begin by dividing into small groups. Each group will spend three to six minutes at each of ten "prayer workout stations." You will need to establish ten prayer stations in ten separate locations. Chairs can be set up in circles at each station so that kids can kneel in front of them to pray. The chairs can also serve as desks for the kids to write on. Each station will have its own "Prayer Station Card" (see pages 53-57).

Be sure to have enough copies of each card for everyone to get one at each station.

An adult should be posted at each station, or with each group, to guide the kids through each of the stations. At each station kids receive a card to direct their prayer time while they are there. Leaders will want to encourage kids to write additional items on their prayer cards. You also may want to add items to some or all of the cards.

PICTURING FORGIVENESS

Directions: Look up each of the following Bible passages. After reading each of them, list as many word pictures about how God forgives our sins as possible next to each of the verses.

Example: 1 John 1:9

Word Picture: Putting clothes with sin written all over them in a washing machine.

Bible Passage:	Word Picture:
"You forgave the iniquity of your people and covered all their sins" Psalm 85:2.	
"For as high as the heavens are above the earth, so great is his love for those who fear him; as far as the east is from the west, so far has he removed our transgressions from us" Psalm 103:11-12.	
"Surely it was for my benefit that I suffered such anguish. In your love you kept me from the pit of destruction; you have put all my sins behind your back" Isaiah 38:17.	
"I, even I, am he who blots out your transgressions, for my own sake, and remembers your sins no more" Isaiah 43:25.	
"I have swept away your offences like a cloud, your sins like the morning mist. Return to me, for I have redeemed you" Isaiah 44:22.	
"Who is a God like you, who pardons sin and forgives the transgression of the remnant of his inheritance? You do not stay angry forever but delight to show mercy. You will again have compassion on us; you will tread our sins underfoot and hurl all our iniquities into the depths of the sea" Micah 7:18-19.	
"When you were dead in your sins and in the uncircumcision of your sinful nature, God made you alive with Christ. He forgave us all our sins, having canceled the written code, with its regulations, that was against us and that stood opposed to us; he took it away, nailing it to the cross" Colossians 2:13.	
"If we confess our sins, he is faithful and just and will forgive us our sins and purify us from all unrighteousness" 1 John 1:9.	

STATION 1—PRAISE

"I will praise you, O Lord, with all my heart; I will tell of all your wonders. I will be glad and rejoice in you; I will sing praise to your name, O Most High" Psalm 9:1–2.

Praise God because he is:

Able	Great	Majestic	Satisfying
Awesome	Generous	Merciful	Sufficient
Acceptable	Glorious	Pure	Truth
Beautiful	Gracious	Patient	Timeless
Creator	Holy	Present	Trustworthy
Complete	Healing	Peaceful	Unique
Changeless	Honorable	Powerful	Victorious
Compassionate	Infinite	Radiant	Wise
Eternal	Invincible	Reliable	Worthy
Exalted	Just	Righteous	Wonderful
Excellent	Joyful	Responsive	(Fill in your own descriptions in the blanks below)
Fair	Kind	Saving	
Faithful	Knowing	Secure	_____
Forgiving	Loving	Stable	_____
Friendly	Limitless	Strong	_____

STATION 2—FOCUS ON JESUS

"Worthy is the Lamb, who was slain, to receive power and wealth and wisdom and strength and honor and glory and praise!" Revelation 5:12b.

Meditate on the names of Jesus and thank him for being: (Circle 5 of the following)

Advocate	Good Shepherd	Lamb of God
Almighty	Head of the Church	King
Alpha and Omega	Jehovah	Righteous One
Beloved Son	Light of the World	Jesus
Bread of Life	Only-Begotten Son	Immanuel
Author of Salvation	Prince of Peace	I Am
Chief Shepherd	Rock	Holy One
Christ of God	Word	Holy Child
Counselor	Savior	Lord of All
Creator	Beginning & End	Lord of Lords
Deliverer	Son of Man	Ruler
Gate	Truth	(Fill in your own descriptions in the blanks below)
Chosen of God	Son of God	
Everlasting Father	Prophet	_____
Faithful Witness	Mighty One	_____
Glory of the Lord	Mighty God	_____
Son of the Most High	Mediator	

STATION 3—THANKSGIVING

"Be joyful always; pray continually; give thanks in all circumstances, for this is God's will for you in Christ Jesus" 1 Thessalonians 5:16–18.

Thank God for your:

Life   Health
Faith
Love   Family
Food   School
Church   Friends

STATION 4—FORGIVENESS

"If we confess our sins, he is faithful and just and will forgive us our sins and purify us from all unrighteousness" 1 John 1:9.

Silently ask God to forgive you for any sin or wrongdoing. You can use the following questions to help you do this.

1. Have you ever done something your parents did not want you to do?
2. Have you ever talked badly about someone when they did not know about it?
3. Have you ever taken something that did not belong to you?
4. Have you ever wanted something really badly even though you knew you could not have it?
5. Have you ever lied?
6. Have you ever been mean to someone?
7. Have you ever been jealous of what someone else had?
8. Have you ever talked back to your parents?
9. Have you ever cheated on a spelling test?
10. Have you ever cared about yourself more than you cared about anyone else?
11. Write out another one here: _____

STATION 5—OUR CHURCH

"We ought always to thank God for you, brothers, and rightly so, because your faith is growing more and more, and the love every one of you has for each other is increasing. Therefore, among God's churches we boast about your perserverence and faith in all the persecutions and trials you are enduring"
2 Thessalonians 1:3–4.

Name the pastors you will pray for:

List church activities you will pray for:

Name the church leaders you will pray for:

List our church's missionaries you will pray for:

Name our group leaders you will pray for:

List our group activities you will pray for:

NOW PRAY FOR EACH OF THESE!

STATION 6—EACH OTHER

"And pray in the Spirit on all occasions with all kinds of prayers and requests. With this in mind, be alert and always keep on praying for all the saints"
Ephesians 6:18.

Write, in each of these boxes below, a name of someone in or out of our group that you will pray for:

NOW PRAY FOR EACH OF THEM!

STATION 7—GOD'S PROTECTION

"And pray that we may be delivered from wicked and evil men, for not everyone has faith. But the Lord is faithful, and he will strengthen and protect you from the evil one" 2 Thessalonians 3:2–3.

Pray for God's strength and protection in choosing the right kinds of friends.

Pray for God's strength and protection while you are at school.

Pray for God's strength and protection as you grow with your family.

Pray for God's strength and protection in the sports you play.

Pray for God's strength and protection in choosing what you do with your free time.

Pray for God's strength and protection . . . (complete the sentence) . . .

STATION 8—THE GOSPEL'S SPREAD

"I pray that you may be active in sharing the faith, so that you will have a full understanding of every good thing we have in Christ" Philemon 6.

Read each of the following verses quietly to yourself. Then pray using the prayer instructions found after each verse.

"He said to them, 'Go into all the world and preach the good news to all creation' " Mark 16:15.
Pray that the Good News of God's salvation will be heard by all of your friends.

"He commanded us to preach to the people and to testify that he is the one whom God appointed as judge of the living and the dead. All the prophets testify about him that everyone who believes in him receives forgiveness of sins through his name" Acts 10:42–43.
Pray that you can be a witness to your friends about God's plan of salvation.

"Pray also for me, that whenever I open my mouth, words may be given me so that I will fearlessly make known the mystery of the gospel, for which I am an ambassador in chains. Pray that I may declare it fearlessly, as I should" Philippians 6:19–20.
Pray for courage in talking about Christ with your friends.

STATION 9 — SPECIAL CONCERNS

"Do not be anxious about anything, but in everything, by prayer and petition, with thanksgiving, present your requests to God. And the peace of God, which transcends all understanding, will guard your hearts and your minds in Christ Jesus" Philippians 4:6–7.

In the boxes below make a list of any special concerns you or others in your group feel need prayer.

STATION 10 — JUST PRAY!

"Let us then approach the throne of grace with confidence, so that we may receive mercy and find grace to help us in our time of need" Hebrews 4:16.

Ask the Lord to put something on your heart, write it down here and then pray about it!

Teaching Energizers

Designed to enhance your teaching, many of these creative activities manage to challenge your young audience and entertain them at the same time.

Activity Hunt

Keeping your kids on the move can liven up any Sunday school lesson or meeting time. Prepare your lesson in advance by breaking the meeting's activities into separate parts that can be carried out in different rooms or meeting areas. Have adult leaders stationed at each of the locations (the number will depend on how many parts you break the lesson or meeting into). At each spot, plan an activity that a team of kids must complete before moving on to the next location.

Each team should receive a separate list of the locations. All teams go to every location, but not in the same order. Once the activity in an area is completed, the adult leader signs the list and the team moves on to the next location. Activities can be totally wild or educational (perhaps related to the theme of your meeting). It may even be possible to combine the two. One example might be having team members stand on their heads while memorizing a verse of Scripture.

Biblical Time Machine

The notion of a "Biblical Time Machine" may help make a Bible story come to life. Using some imagination, you or your kids can identify a location in your church that can simulate the environment found in the Bible story you are studying. Then pretend to take a trip back in time and study the story in this special location. For example, if you were studying the story of Jonah and the whale you could go into a small room in the church's basement. For Daniel in the lion's den, you could create a den using a tarp over folding chairs. If you were examining the temptation of Christ by Satan in the desert, you might go outside and walk around the church parking lot while doing the study. This technique can help kids think more carefully about the historical context of a story.

Car-azy Bible Study

Try conducting your next Bible study in cars. That's right, automobiles (four-door models are preferable). Make sure all the emergency brakes are on and appoint at least one Safety Guard. With four kids to a car, supply each car with Bibles and whatever lesson guide(s) you are using. The primary rule for the study is to let only the person in the driver's seat talk. If kids have questions they want to ask, they must wait until it is their turn in the driver's seat. You can signal kids, every five to ten minutes, to rotate seats clockwise within the car; a loud whistle or horn works well. With each rotation, the person in the driver's

seat takes over as leader.

The rotation can also move from car to car. Once a person rotates into the left rear seat of a car, they then rotate out of their original car into the driver's seat of another car when the whistle blows.

Should this get boring after a while, blowing the whistle two or three times in succession will force everyone to move around to different cars quickly!

Such round-robin discussions are sure to be lively. The person with the whistle or horn can control how fast or how slow the study is to progress. A similar format can be followed indoors or outdoors using chairs, but it really is more fun in the church parking lot.

Cryptoquip

Getting your kids excited about looking at Scripture can sometimes seem impossible. "Cryptoquipping" may be the trick to helping young and old alike learn and memorize Scripture truths and promises. A "quip" can also be used to introduce a Sunday school lesson, fellowship topic, or Bible study. Here's an example of how it works:

Py Ay Yakdqn Fn Oyw Rywip Kfzd Akdx Py Ay Oyw. Iwbd 6:31.

Clues: A = T D = E F = A O = Y P = D

This cryptoquip is a simple substitution cipher in which each letter stands for another. If you find that Y=O, it will be that way throughout the puzzle. The solution is accomplished by trial and error. One hint is to use short words to get clues for locating the vowels. The age of your group will determine the number of "equal-to" clues you give them to start with.

You can create your own cryptoquips by listing the letters of the alphabet vertically down a page and then randomly assigning a new letter to each one. The following cryptoquip alphabet was created to scramble the sample verse above.

A = T	J = C	S = B
B = K	K = H	T = J
C = N	L = F	U = P
D = E	M = Z	V = X
E = G	N = S	W = U
F = A	O = Y	X = M
G = Q	P = D	Y = O
H = I	Q = R	Z = V
I = L	R = W	

After trying the example above, make up cryptoquips for other verses. Be careful to double-check your letters for accuracy (kids will never let you forget it if you make an error). By the way, this sample quip is found in Luke 6:31.

Lesson Recollection

Most people have difficulty retaining even the main point of a single sermon or lesson. To overcome this obstacle to learning, try using a visual collage of knickknacks to help kids recall a series of lessons. At the start of a month long or quarter long series of lessons, place a sheet of poster board in your regular meeting room. Each week bring an object that symbolizes the main point for the week's lesson. A salt packet from a fast-food restaurant might work for a lesson from Matthew 5 ("You are the salt of the earth"). Monopoly money might represent a lesson from 2 Corinthians 9 ("God loves a cheerful giver"). At the end

of the lesson, attach the object to the poster board.

The growing collage of miscellaneous items may look like a collection of junk, but to your kids it will have special meaning. At the beginning of each week's lesson, they are sure to associate the posted objects with the corresponding lessons and soon they may even feel some ownership of the board and want to make their own additions. The visual continuity of a lesson-recall board can also give the group a sense of history and belonging.

No-Risk Discussion

Kids can be intimidated easily when asked to express opinions in front of their peers, especially on difficult issues. The "no-risk" approach presented here may enable them to say what they feel without fear of what others might think. Begin by giving each of your group members a sheet of paper and a pencil. Ask everyone to write a Number 1 near the top of the paper. Then, using questions formulated in advance, ask everyone to write out an answer to the first question. Questions should be such that they can be answered in a sentence or two. Participants then fold their papers down and over to conceal the answers and pass the papers to the person on their left. Question Number 2 is then asked. Participants write their answer to the second question right below the folded-down portion. With each question, the paper is folded and passed to a new person until all the questions have been answered. Be sure to tell kids that it is okay to leave a question blank if they do not have a response.

Once the questions are all answered, the papers are collected. You can then read different kids' responses and discuss them further without revealing whose opinion is whose. Usually this format leads to further, less-inhibited discussion, especially when the young people discover that their views are shared by others in the group. (Young people are conscious of their penmanship so it is best if *you* read the papers.)

Picture Pages

This is a creative take-off on "Picture Pages," the short takes that have aired on the Nickelodeon Cable Network. It is a way of helping kids remember Scripture by drawing a picture. Even simple stick drawings can implant ideas in a young person's mind better than anything you might say.

Buy a large sketch pad, or use large pieces of newsprint. Study the passage you are planning to talk about and get a feel for the biblical truth you want to focus on. Then start drawing.

Here is an example of how you might use drawings for Colossians 2:6-7:

So then, just as you **received** Christ Jesus as Lord, continue to live in him, **rooted** and **built** up in him, **strengthened** in the faith as you were taught, and **overflowing** with thankfulness.

You might have five drawings for this passage—the words **received** (maybe a person receiving an award), **rooted** (a tree), **built** (a house), **strengthened** (an athlete lifting weights), and **overflowing** (a broken toilet).

You can also write the key words at the bottom of each page and have the group call out suggestions for pictures to be drawn. If you have artistic kids in the group, let them do the drawings. The group will have fun with this and they will get a firmer grasp on the meaning of the passage being studied.

Sense Scriptures

One way to add some depth to studying a passage of scripture is to have kids use their imaginations and relate what their senses might experience if they were actually a part of the story. Begin by reading the passage to the group. Then ask them to close their eyes as you read the passage a second time. Encourage them to try and "sense" from the story or situation what they might see, hear, smell, taste, and feel if they were actually there. You want them to imagine themselves inside the scene of the incident as it is described in the passage. Then ask the group to share what their senses would tell them about the story.

For example, when Jesus calmed the storm in Matthew 8, responses might sound like this:

SEE—dark clouds, lightning, big waves, sea gulls.

HEAR—thunder, splashing, men hollering, boat creaking.

TASTE—water, salt, cottonmouth (fear), lunch coming up.

FEEL—seasick, the boat rocking, the humidity, the cold.

SMELL—rain, salt, wet people who smell bad, fish. On the "feel" part, you might want to consider emotional feelings as well—fear, anger (because Jesus was sleeping), confusion, frustration, and so on.

Sitcom Discussions

To encourage discussion and creative thinking about any topic, capitalize on kids' interest in television. Find out from your kids which of the popular TV situation comedies they watch. Divide the kids into small groups of four to six and ask each group to take a different sitcom and dramatize the topic they are currently studying, using the characters and formats from the sitcoms. The groups would decide how their favorite characters would react to the topic and what they would say. If the topic was honesty and the group's sitcom was *The Cosby Show*, they would act out a typical scene from that program, playing the show's characters. In the process they would communicate tips, warnings, or whatever about honesty. Discussion of the topic would follow after the group's performance.

Spotlight Meeting

In a darkened room, have kids sit in a large circle. Give one person (either an adult or young person) a flashlight to serve as the "spotlight." It is used to light up individual faces in the circle. Only the person in the "spotlight" can speak. The first round is usually a simple word association (or some other nonthreatening game) to get kids loosened up and into the spirit of things. The person with the flashlight starts the round with an initial word and then "spotlights" one person at a time. The person in the light must answer with a word associated with the word voiced by the person before them.

In the second round, the "spotlighter" asks each person one question that they are to answer as honestly as possible. The spotlight draws everyone's attention to that one person and can be a very effective way for kids to share with each other. Questions can be deep or shallow depending on what seems appropriate for the group. Questions should be designed to allow kids to honestly express themselves and their faith without fear or embarrassment. Individuals should have the option to "pass" if they don't want to answer a question.

Tape Talk

Taped interviews with people outside the group can be one way of helping kids consider different viewpoints on a given topic. Using a cassette recorder, interviews can be conducted by kids or leaders and brought back to the group to share and discuss. The interviews need not be long and may involve only a single question about the topic being studied. They could be conducted at church with known adults or at a local mall with strangers. Whatever the subject, the interview results are certain to spark discussion as kids listen to the opinions and comments of others.

Triangular Teaching

Teaching can be enhanced considerably by making minor changes in how a room is set up. The following arrangement is ideal for teaching about any topic that has three distinct points. A subject like the Trinity is perfect for this setup.

Arrange the chairs in a triangle, so that they are facing toward the middle.

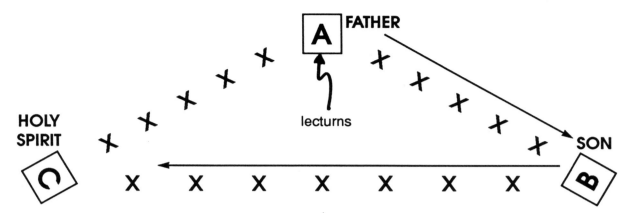

At each corner of the triangle, place a speaker's stand. When you get to the first point in your lesson (God the Father), you stand in corner A. When you come to the second point (God the Son), you move to corner B. Finally, you move on to corner C for the third point (the Holy Spirit). During the discussion that follows the lesson, maintain the same pattern in moving from corner to corner, depending on which point you are discussing. The altered physical arrangement, along with your movement around the room, will serve to keep kids' interest during the lesson.

Faith Sparkers

Here you will find a number of special activities structured to promote young people's understanding of God and to strengthen their relationship to him.

Just as Jesus used commonplace things to communicate truths about God, this exercise can encourage kids to think about the nature of God by using everyday objects and a format they are very familiar with. Before meeting with your kids, gather up a small collection of ordinary objects—a light bulb, a coat hanger, a roll of tape, a bar of soap. At the meeting, divide kids into small groups and give each group one of the objects. Each group must then compose a one-line slogan, like those used in commercials, to describe how God is like the object they have been given. If the object is a light bulb, the group might come up with "God is like a light bulb—he lights up my life!" If it is a roll of tape they might suggest that "God is like a roll of tape—he holds the world together!"

This exercise can provide an opportunity to discuss the various images of God and to consider how to start looking for God in everyday things. It might also be a prime time to look at some biblical examples of spiritual truths illustrated through ordinary things, like "The kingdom of God is like a wheat field . . . ."

Balloon Worship

Give each person in your group a balloon and a slip of paper as they enter for a group worship service. As a call to worship, ask everyone to write on their paper something nice that they might say to someone else. Such things as "I love you," "I think you are great," and "You are special" would be appropriate. Then ask everyone to roll up their papers and place them inside the balloons. The balloons can then be blown up and tied. Ask the group to hold on to the balloons until the offering portion of the service.

When it is time for the offering, the worship leader asks everyone to bat their balloons forward as an offering to God, the messages being their gifts to the Lord. Then, as the service ends, the leader asks the participants to come to the front, to take a balloon, and to pop it. The message they receive in the balloon serves as the benediction for the ser-

vice, as a message to them from God.

Note: Amidst the confusion at the end, some balloons may get broken. To ensure that everyone gets a balloon to pop, leaders should prepare two or three extras.

Circle Prayer of Sharing

While group members stand in a loose circle with hands at their sides, the leader explains that this is to be a time of sharing prayers about friendship. Everyone is invited, but not required, to share their thoughts. The leader opens with several prayer thoughts about friendship and then takes the hand of the person on his or her left. The person on the leader's left adds his or her own thoughts and takes the hand of the person next to the left. The process is repeated until everyone is holding hands. If a person does not wish to contribute, he or she just takes the hand of the person on his or her left. At the end, the leader concludes with some comments about the value of sharing in friendship and how the circle formed now includes everyone.

Door Jammin'

This activity can serve as a physical reminder of the decisions young people have made for Christ. The event is best begun with a review of several Bible passages that talk about doorposts (doorjambs) and doors (e.g., Exodus 11 and

12:13, Deuteronomy 6:4-9, Revelation 3:20). The group can then spend some time talking about the verses' meanings and how they relate to the "door of faith" discussed in Acts 14:26-27.

Then have the group make its own door of faith! Give new converts (and old) permanent ink pens and ask them to write their names and the dates of their commitment to Christ on the door-jambs of your meeting room. If they cannot remember a specific date, have them pick a date that is close. Each time group members pass through the door they will be reminded of the new and old Christians in their group and of what the Lord has done for them.

A God's Eye View

Used in conjunction with Psalm 8, the following narrative dramatically illustrates the majesty of God's creation. It is also a good image booster as it reminds kids of their significance in God's eyes.

I want you to use your imagination. Imagine that I have a long sheet of paper that stretches all the way across the front of the room, out the door, outside the building, and continues until you can't see it anymore.

Now imagine that I take a pin and poke a tiny hole in the paper to represent the earth. All the cities, mountains, and oceans of our planet are represented by that speck.

About five-eighths of an inch from the pinhole, I make another pinhole to represent the moon.

Now imagine that nineteen feet away, I draw a two-inch circle that is the sun. Six hundred feet away—the length of two football fields—we come to Neptune.

After leaving the solar system and our pinhole planets, we would have to travel along a thousand miles of paper to come to the nearest star. That is roughly the distance between Chicago and Denver.

Distances in space are so vast they are measured in light-years, the distance that light will travel in a year. Light travels at over 186,000 miles per second. That is so fast that a bullet shot at that speed and circling the earth would hit you seven times before you fell to the ground, even if it took you one second to fall.

At the speed of light, you could travel from Los Angeles to New York in one-sixtieth of a second. You could reach the moon in less than one and a half seconds, the sun in eight minutes, and cover the entire solar system in eleven hours.

But even at those speeds, it would take you 4.3 years to reach the nearest star. You would need 400 years to reach the North Star; and to cross just one galaxy, our own Milky Way, would take 120,000 years. And astronomers now estimate that there are over 100 million galaxies.

After reading the narrative to the group, you might want to have the kids read Psalm 8 in unison. With this as a background, you can discuss the following questions or other questions of your choice.

1. How does this Psalm make you feel about God?
2. How does this Psalm make you feel about yourself?
3. What does this Psalm suggest a person's self-image should be? (See also Matthew 10:29-33.)
4. What do you think it means when the Psalmist says that God crowned humanity with love and honor?
5. Why do you think God needed to create such a large universe?

Godzilla Meets the Group

Providing an opportunity for your kids to get to know the various leaders within your church can help them feel more a part of the Body of Christ. A simple invitation to have church elders or other leaders come visit with your children's group is all it takes. A sample letter is provided below.

Dear _____ ,

Our kids are growing up. Along with this maturity comes lots of questions about themselves, God, the church, its leaders, their homes, friends, and lots of other areas. Because of this, I think it is important that the leaders of our church occasionally share personally with our young people. I would like to provide this opportunity on _____ .

I would like for you to be able to share in what we might want to call "Our Kids Meet Godzilla." (Hey, that's supposed to be funny!) Often they see the leaders as powerful and terrifying creatures. As adults that may seem funny, but for kids it's too often true.

I would like for you to take about six or seven minutes to share with them about your job, your family, your background, how long you have been a Christian, and one area you are presently working to strengthen in your Christian life.
In Christ,

You might also assign these leaders a particular topic to talk about. Possibilities might include things like "What I do when I blow it," "What I wish someone had told me when I was in fifth grade," or "What you have to look forward to." Then, be sure to allow time for kids to ask questions or to discuss the issues that were raised by the adults. Planning for this kind of exchange, once or twice a year, can help to build community within the church and will help both age groups to appreciate each other more.

Grill the Pastor

Helping kids to understand the role of a pastor in the church's life is not always easy. They often see only the pulpit personality who preaches and officiates at worship services. Having the pastor visit your group for an informal question-and-answer session can improve their perceptions of the person behind the role. Just having the pastor appear in casual attire will change some of their misconceptions.

Work with the kids beforehand to prepare some questions that can be written out on three-by-five cards. They may at first feel shy about asking their visitor questions, so having some on hand will get the session started. Encourage kids to think up their own questions, but don't hesitate to use the suggestions provided below.

- What do you especially enjoy about being a pastor?
- What kind of books do you enjoy reading?
- How do you go about putting together a sermon?
- Where did you grow up? What was it like there?
- What is one of your favorite parts of the Bible?
- What kind of music do you like?
- What kinds of things did kids do when you were our age?
- What do you like to do in your spare time?
- What are a few of your favorite movies or TV shows?
- If you were not a pastor, what would your second career choice be?
- What do you say to a person who just had one of their family die?
- How many marriages and funerals do you conduct during the year?
- Who would you consider to be your personal heroes?
- What advice can you give us about our group?

Before the meeting is over, you might let the pastor ask a few questions of the group as well. This type of meeting can encourage positive feelings between the pastor and the kids, especially when a pastor is new.

How God Sees Me

Provide each person with a sheet of newsprint. On one side have them draw pictures, cartoons, or sayings expressing "How I See God." Then have them fill the other side with symbols expressing "How I Think God Sees Me." Allow ten to twenty minutes to complete both sides.

When everyone is finished, ask each person to explain his or her drawing to the group. This exercise opens the group to sharing about where they are at with God. It can also demonstrate the varying facets of any one individual's experience with God.

Letters to Jesus

Praying in a group can be awkward for many young people. Having limited

experience with conversational prayer, they often feel inadequate and can be easily intimidated if asked to pray out loud. This exercise is designed to help kids overcome some of the awkwardness by writing out their prayers to Jesus.

Give everyone pencils, paper, and some idea of what a prayer letter should include. Suggest, for example, that the letter begin with greetings and some personal thank-you's. Kids can thank him for someone or for something, and they can tell Jesus why they appreciate him. Suggest that they write about some experience they have had lately, a time when they felt happy or when they felt lousy. They might also write out some of their concerns and worries. If they have any prayer requests, they can write those out as well.

After the kids have had time to write their letters, explain that these letters are just like prayers and that God actually does get them. Suggest that reading the letters out loud, either in the group or at home alone, is just like "mailing" them to God. If the youngsters seem willing, you might ask them to share their letters with each other. Of course, kids should be allowed to pass if they want to.

Love Is

One simple way to get kids involved in an object lesson on the subject of love is to hang a large, heart-shaped piece of poster board on the wall. Write on the heart the words, "Love Is." Over a period of several weeks, have kids write their definitions of love all over the heart. Some will be frivolous, but taken together they can provide an excellent springboard for discussion.

Our Group Coat of Arms

Creating a group coat of arms can allow your kids to expressively voice their feelings about the group. It offers an opportunity to talk with your group about its good characteristics and how the group feels it might be improved.

Photocopy multiple copies of the handout "Our Group Coat of Arms" found on the following page. Give one copy to each group member and explain that a "coat of arms" is a name shield with emblems or symbols that characterize the good qualities about a person and his or her family. Their task is to symbolically represent the group's good qualities. The instructions below can facilitate the activity, or you can identify your own items to be included in the coat of arms.

Instructions: Use paints, crayons, or markers to decorate your coat of arms. There are six spaces to be filled.
1. Symbolize something our group has done for others in the past.
2. Symbolize the purpose of our group.
3. Draw what you think the most important activity of our group is.
4. Draw a picture of our group's greatest achievement.
5. Symbolize how you feel God sees our group.
6. Include three words that should be most important to our group.

OUR GROUP COAT OF ARMS

Parent Opinions

Give your kids a "question of the week" to take home. Their assignment is to get their parents' answers to the question. Let the kids in the group come up with the questions, giving them examples to consider. The answers to questions like "What is the most important goal in your life?" or "What gives you the greatest satisfaction in life?" or "What do you think about all the violence on TV?" will open discussions between kids and their parents, and will also provide excellent material for a group discussion in which kids compare parents' answers with their own.

Popcorn Prayers

Group prayer isn't always easy for young people. "Popcorn prayers" are simple phrases or one-word responses to a leader's directions for kids to voice how they feel about God, the church, themselves, or a particular event. Examples of such prayers could be: "Thank you," "Great," "Warmth," "Together," "Love," and "Growing."

Progressive Worship Service

Organized along the lines of a progressive dinner, this worship activity can serve to help kids understand the various elements of a worship service. The format is such that it can be done in a church, in homes, or as part of a weekend retreat.

Dividing up the different parts of a worship service, arrange to conduct each one in a separate location—a different room or a different home. The number of locations is variable. One possible sequencing of parts is suggested below, using Acts 2:42 and Colossians 3:16 as a scriptural foundation.

- *Fellowship:* Begin with some kind of group interaction or sharing to provide kids with a chance to get to know one another better.
- *Spiritual Songs:* At the next location, have someone lead the group in a variety of well-known hymns and favorite songs of worship.
- *Prayer:* Move to another location that provides a good atmosphere for prayer. An outside garden can be an ideal location, reminiscent of Christ's prayer in garden settings. Have several kids lead in prayer, responding to requests and offering thanksgiving to God. If your group of kids is not in the habit of voicing spontaneous prayers out loud, you could spend a few minutes having them write out their prayers or guiding them through a time of silent prayer.
- *Scripture Reading:* At the next location, have several kids read lessons from the Old Testament, the New Testament, and perhaps the Psalms. Use a modern English translation.
- *Teaching:* The next stop can be for a traditional sermon. Or it can involve teaching through another medium

such as a film, a play, or a structured dialogue.

- *Breaking of Bread (Communion):* The last stop can be around the Lord's table, with a communion service. Be sure to make it a time of celebration and joy.

There are, of course, other ingredients that are part of regular worship services (like the offering). These can be incorporated into another segment of worship or they can be handled independently at a separate location. It is best to design your own worship service, keeping in mind your church's format for worship. Whatever the structure, a progressive worship service can be one of the group's more memorable events.

Scripture Memory Helps

Motivating kids to memorize God's Word requires taking the time to help them feel capable in their efforts. The following activity may provide a starting point in discussing the value of Scripture memorization and the hints for doing it successfully.

As an introduction, give all the kids pencils and paper and ask them to write down the following pieces of information:

- Their name
- Their address
- Their phone number
- Their room number at school
- Their birth date
- Phone numbers of three friends
- Addresses of three friends
- First verse of a favorite song
- Three Bible verses

When they are done, let the kids have fun sharing answers to the first nine questions. Then comment on how Scripture memory takes a back seat to many relatively trivial details and use the following questions to generate a discussion about Scripture memory:

- How were you able to remember phone numbers, addresses, and others items on the list?
- Have you ever used those same

methods to memorize Scripture?
- Do you need to memorize God's Word?

Consider this! After twenty-four hours we remember five percent of what we hear (Romans 1:15-17), fifteen percent of what we read (Revelation 1:3), thirty-five percent of what we study (Acts 17:11), and one hundred percent of what we memorize (Psalm 119:11). Studying the following Scriptures may help to reinforce the value of memorization:

Psalm 119:9, 11
Matthew 4:1-11
Joshua 1:8
2 Timothy 3:16-17
Ephesians 6:11-13, 17
Hebrews 4:12
Romans 10:17
Romans 12:2
Philippians 4:8

Conclude the discussion by sharing some of the following hints for memorizing Scripture. You might also ask the group for other possible hints and suggestions.

- Choose a verse that is special to you. Read and study the verse until you know what it means.
- Meditate on the verse. Think it over

again and again until it becomes part of you.

- Write out the verse and reference a number of times.
- Categorize verses. 1 John 5:11-13, for example, could be under an "assurance of salvation" heading.
- When memorizing, quote the topic, the reference, and the verse.
- Break the verse down into smaller phrases and work on memorizing one phrase at a time until you finish the entire verse.
- Start working on a new verse before you go to bed at night. You tend to remember what you are thinking about just before you fall asleep.
- Write out the verses on spiral-bound, three-by-five index cards so you can carry them with you and work on them wherever you go.
- Use time that is often wasted, such as traveling to and from school, during meals, while exercising or jogging. This is an especially good way to memorize the books of the Bible. Instead of counting push-ups, recite the Bible books (you just may be able to increase your push-up maximum because you will have no mental block as you often do when you approach a certain number).
- Accountability! Work with a partner to whom you can be accountable. Check up on each other and quiz each other.
- Set a goal (one or two verses a week, for example); then reward yourself or your partner when either or both of you consistently accomplish your goals over a one- or two-month period.
- Review, review, review. If you do not use the verses regularly, you will lose them.

Singing Worship Service

In an attempt to put more meaning into the songs your kids sing in church, spend one or more meetings letting the group members request their favorites, one at a time. The catch is, they must also share with the group why the song is meaningful before it is sung. Having hymnals or song books available will help get things started.

Thank-You Notes to God

Young people are often much better at writing out their thoughts than at expressing them verbally. This written exercise can be very useful whenever you want to encourage kids to express their thanks to God for his many gifts.

Provide your group with some purchased thank-you cards or notepaper and ask them to write out a thank-you letter to God. This might be done as part of a time of meditation or after a Bible reading that focuses on the giving nature of God. Once the letters are written, ask a few volunteers to share their letters with the group.

The Tie That Binds

Working with a group of no more than thirty, ask participants to stand in a circle. Then take a long, thick piece of rope or cord and loop it around each person, using the illustration as a guide. Then, without explaining the purpose, have kids take a large step backward, one at a time. (Usually about halfway around the circle someone will get the bright idea to give a good squeeze to a neighbor; allow this to happen.) When everyone has stepped back, the rope can be dropped and everyone can sit down for the discussion.

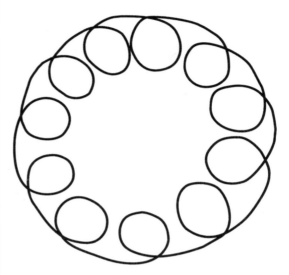

Talk about what happened when group members stepped back, both to themselves and to the people around them. Point out that the rope symbolizes the love that must exist between all of Jesus' disciples (John 13:35). This love for one another must bind them together as the rope did: It is the "tie that binds" all Christians together. Discussion may touch on what happens when a person tries to break away from fellowship, and on the role of love in holding that person in. As the discussion comes to an end, you might close by singing "Blest Be the Tie That Binds."

Translating the Lord's Prayer

Whether or not your group is familiar with the Lord's Prayer, this exercise will assist them in understanding its deepest meanings in a personal way.

As a first step toward developing their own translation of the Lord's Prayer, have the kids look at and compare the two passages in the New Testament that contain the Lord's Prayer (Matthew 6:9-13 and Luke 11:2-4). They can discuss the similarities and differences between the two versions.

The second step is to compare the passages in different translations of the Bible. Have the group read out loud at least three different translations and discuss the distinctions between the different versions.

Now, with the research done, have kids individually compose and write out their own versions of the Lord's Prayer. Suggest that they start by selecting from the various translations already studied those words and phrases that are most meaningful for them.

After everyone is finished, have kids share their translations with each other. Working together, have them vote or agree by consensus on a group translation that best combines their understanding of the Lord's Prayer.

The group translation could then be

used in a regular worship service accompanied by an explanation from the group about how and why it composed the prayer translation this way.

Yarn Circle

This activity can be used as part of a communion service or to reinforce a time of sharing. Ask kids to be seated in a circle, either on the floor or in chairs. Give each person a piece of yarn, about eighteen inches long. The yarn is to represent their individuality. Then ask the group to share with each other about some aspect of their lives. Once they have shared, tell them to tie their string to that of someone on either side of them. Explain that this is to symbolize the unity of the group and the fact that we are all one in Christ. The group may then enter into a time of reflection on Christ, the cross, the resurrection, or the Lord's Supper.

To close, the leader goes to each person and cuts off a section of the string, leaving one knot on each person's section to represent the change that has happened during the experience. The piece of string that the young person receives represents the fact that we leave the meeting as individuals, but at the same we belong to the body of Christ and are connected to others in the group.

Quick-Plan Special Events

Some are wild and some are crazy. They are all sure to transform a social or fellowship activity into a memorable event.

Backward Night

Here is an evening of activities where everything runs in reverse. Invitations and posters can be printed backward (even from bottom to top), and oral announcements can be made with one's back to the audience. Tell everyone to come with their clothes on backward and inside out.

As the kids arrive, have them use the back door of the church or meeting place. Appropriate signs, spelled backward, can be placed at the regular entrance, directing them to the rear. Greet them at the door with "Good-bye, hope you had a good time" and other such salutations. The program itself can be run exactly in reverse. Begin with a devotional if you usually have one at the conclusion. As the kids leave, put name tags on them, welcome them, and introduce visitors. If paper plates are used for refreshments, use them upside down, and make everyone eat left-handed (if they are right-handed). Or go one step further and include a "Regressive Dinner" as part of the evening's events.

Supply List:
Name tags
Small slips of paper (for charades)

4 sets of cards with the letters
   B-A-C-K-W-A-R-D
Paper cups—one per team

Explanation:
Divide the group into at least four teams of five to seven people. Subtract points for the winners, rather than awarding points. (Have each team begin with 10,000 points, then they lose points as they win.) The team names can be barnyard animals. The team members must then make the noise of their animal during the games, but the sounds must be made in reverse. For example, a donkey would go "Haw-Hee," a dog would go "Wow-Bow," and a cow would go "Ooooom." Select several of the following backward games, or you might try playing your group's favorite game(s) in reverse, using the suggestions here as guidelines.

Back-to-Back Relay: This is a variation of the old "Three-Legged Race." Rather than tying two people side by side, you put two people back to back and have them interlock arms. During the relay one of them runs forward, and the other runs backward. When the two players reach the finish line, instead of turning around to run back, the one who ran forward now runs backward. When one pair finishes, the next pair goes. The first team to finish is the winner.

Backward Letter Scramble: Prepare ahead of time four sets of cards (one set for each team) with the letters B-A-C-K-W-A-R-D on them. In other words, each team gets eight cards. The cards are passed out to the various team members. You then call out certain words that can be spelled using those letters.

The first team to get in line, spelling the word *backward* is the winner. Words to use include: backward, drab, rack, ward, raw, ark, back, crab, bard, and so on. If you call out the word *drab* for example, kids with those four letters must quickly line up facing you so that cards spell it *bard.*

Backward Charades: This game is just like regular charades, only the titles must be acted out in reverse. For example, instead of "The Sound of Music," the player must act out "Music of Sound The." Teams must correctly guess the backward titles.

Backward Human Obstacle Course: For this relay, teams line up single file. Ten additional members (or adult workers) serve as the obstacles: a pole to circle around, leg tunnels to go under, kneelers-on-all-fours to leap over, and sitters-with-outstretched-legs to step in among. On the signal, the first persons in line go completely around the pole, under the tunnels, over the kneelers, in and among the sitters (not missing any stepping space), around another pole, and then back to their teams to tag the next runners. And all of this is done moving *backward*. If an obstacle is missed or improperly executed, the runner must repeat that obstacle.

Behind-the-Back Pass: Team members line up shoulder to shoulder. Several objects are then passed down the line from player to player, behind their backs. The first team to pass a certain number of these objects all the way down the line is the winner. For fun, try using cups of water. Spilling is a penalty and points will be added to the score.

Regressive Dinner: Load up the kids in the van or bus and head out for a backward progressive dinner. It is similar to a regular progressive dinner in that the participants travel from location to location and receive one course of their meal at each prearranged stop. The fun part is that the menu is served in reverse. A possible menu might look something like this.

First stop: Dessert and a toothpick.
Second stop: Potato chips.
Third stop: Sandwich.
Fourth stop: Vegetable.
Fifth stop: Salad.
Sixth stop: Soup.
Seventh stop: Appetizer.

Something to drink should be provided at each stop.

Baggin' It

Having lunch together with your group can become expensive and routine. Here are some ideas that will turn a routine lunch together into an event for after church or anytime you choose.

Supply List:
Each person brings her or his own sack lunch
A large blanket
A large garbage bag for cleanup
Plenty of paper bags—small ones for invitations, large grocery bags for games
Gunnysacks or old king-size pillow cases
Paints, markers, glue, yarn
Pens or pencils
Surprise-bag items of your choice

Explanation:
In keeping with the "Baggin' It" theme, invite your group to the event with paper bag invitations. You can send flat paper bags (lunch size) through the mail. Tape the open end shut and address it on one side. Print your message on the other side or enclose it in the bag. Before or after lunch, have the group play one or more of the suggested activities that have a bag theme (see below).

When it's time for lunch, lay a blanket out on the ground (or on the floor if you are inside). Have all the kids empty the contents of their sack lunches on the blanket. Then have the group gather around the blanket, hold it up by the edges, and raise it high as you offer thanks. Then lower the blanket and allow the kids to pick anything they want from the items that are on the blanket. Since everyone needs to eat, have kids take turns choosing one item at a time until all the food is gone.

This type of lunch can be a great opportunity to build community with everyone involved with your group. Try inviting parents, sponsors, or church staff members.

Sack Sign-Up: Here is a good mixer or a quick get-acquainted game. Give participants a small paper sack that they must place over their right hand. They also receive a pen or pencil or marker. When the game starts, all the kids must go around the room and get signatures on their paper sacks, writing with their left hand. All of those who are left-handed should put the paper sack over their left hand and write with their right hand. The first person who obtains signatures from everyone is the winner.

Bag Races: Divide your group into teams of two. Each kid in the pair puts his or her left foot in a gunnysack or pillow case. On your signal, two teams at a time race to the finish line. Winners race winners until there is one championship team. If you decide to use old pillow cases, players must hop more slowly so they don't rip the case.

Bite the Bag: Stand a grocery bag in the middle of the floor and ask everyone to sit in a wide circle around it. One at a time, have each person come to the bag and try to pick it up with just his or her teeth, then return to a standing position. Nothing but the bottoms of a player's feet are ever allowed to touch the floor.

Almost everyone can do this. After everyone has a turn, cut off or fold down an inch or two of the bag. Go around again. With each round shorten the bag further. When a person is no longer able to pick up the bag and stand again, he or she is out. The winner is the one who can pick the bag up without falling down. For safety's sake, especially as the bag gets lower to the ground, you will want to place an adult leader or two on the sides or in front as spotters.

Masks: Using large paper sacks, have kids make the most creative masks they can think of. Have sponsors judge the winners from a variety of categories: scariest, funniest, ugliest, prettiest, and so on.

Surprise Bag Relay: Divide the group into several teams of equal size and appoint Safety Guards. Have the teams line up single file behind a line. Paper bags containing individually wrapped edible items are placed on chairs, one chair per team, some distance from the teams' starting line. At a signal, players in each line run to their team's chair, sit down, reach into the bag without looking, pull out an item, unwrap it, and eat it. When they have swallowed the entire contents of their packages to the satisfaction of the Safety Guards, they then run back to the starting position and tag the next players. Each player must eat whatever is grabbed out of the bag. Suggestions for the surprise bag include:

    A small bag of chips
    Small green onion

Can of warm soda
Raw carrot
Piece of cream cheese
Candy bar
Peanut butter sandwich
An orange
A peanut

There should be nothing that could make the players sick.

Frislympics

Here is a game event that can captivate your group for an entire afternoon or evening. The games require a large area, either indoors or out, and most of them are best played with foam Frisbees, in the interest of safety.

Supply List:
1 foam Frisbee per team
1 tire per team
2 ropes or garden hoses
1 bucket per team
1 wide-mouth quart jar per team
Awards: string, paper plates, and
    markers

Explanation:
What Olympics would be complete without an opening ceremony? "Killer Frisbee" (see below) can be the perfect game to get players in the mood and ready for the games that follow. Once everyone is warmed up and comfortable with each other, the actual competition can begin. You can select any number of games from those listed below to make up your group's Frislympics. After each event give awards to first-, second-, and third-place teams. Plan ahead and be sure to have enough awards for every member of each team. Awards can be made using string, paper plates, and markers (see diagram). Label each of

the awards using markers. At the conclusion of the games, special recognition awards can be given to each of the teams. Possible special award categories could be the best dressed, the best team spirit, and the best technique.

Accuracu Frisbee: Again, using teams of five to seven, the object here is for team members to successfully toss a Frisbee through a tire that is set upright about twenty-five feet away from each team. Positioned behind a line, team members try, one by one, to toss the Frisbee through the tire. The person throwing the Frisbee retrieves it and hands it to the next person in line. The winning team can be the team with the highest number of successful throws, or it can be the team that finishes first in getting every team member to make a successful throw.

Crazy Legs Frisbee: Divide the group into teams of equal size and have them line up single file behind a starting line. Designate a finish line about twenty feet away. Give each team one Frisbee. Team members go one at a time. Placing the Frisbee between their knees, they run to the finish line and toss the Frisbee back to the next person in line. If the Frisbee is not caught, the thrower must go back and do the whole routine over again. The first team with all its members across the finish line wins.

Distance Frisbee: Divide into teams of five to seven kids and line the teams up single file behind a common starting line. Players get three opportunities to throw. Their best throws are marked and measured, the distance being recorded for the team's total. Throwers retrieve the Frisbees after each throw. The team with the farthest total throws wins.

Freestyle Frisbee: This event is for the "hot dogs" in your group. You can have one or two participants from each team demonstrate their best "freestyle" Frisbee throw. This could be around the back, under the leg, over the head, double skip, boomerang, or any other kind of fancy or crazy shot. A panel of "distinguished and expert" judges can determine the winner(s).

Frisbee Attack: Here is an exciting new version of "Frisbee Tag." For starters you will need a playing area with a radius of about forty feet. The game is best played with five to ten players. One person is chosen to be "It" and another is chosen to be the "Frisbee Thrower." "It" is free to move around, while the "Frisbee Thrower" must stand in the middle of the area, preferably on a sturdy chair or table.

The object of the game is for "It" to get the other players out by hitting them (below the neck) with a Frisbee. As the game begins, "It" has at least three soft Frisbees to work with and tries to hit the other players with them. Players that get hit are "frozen" and can no longer move. If "It" misses, the Frisbee can be captured by the other players. Players that capture a Frisbee then seek to get it to the "Frisbee Thrower" in the middle of the field, either by carrying it or by throwing it. The "Frisbee Thrower" is the only one able to "unfreeze" players who have been frozen by "It." This is accomplished by throwing a captured Frisbee to one of the frozen players, who must catch it before it hits the ground. In catching the Frisbee, frozen players may only move one of their feet. If they move both feet or miss the throw they remain frozen. When a player is "unfrozen," he or she rejoins the active players and seeks to give the Frisbee back to the "Frisbee Thrower" to release another frozen player. Meanwhile, "It" continues scrambling around, trying to hit players with Frisbees, intercept captured Frisbees, and so on. The game ends when "It" has frozen everyone and the "Frisbee Thrower" has no more Frisbees to throw.

When working with a larger group of players, more than one person can be "It." Finding the right balance for an even competition may be a matter of trial and error but shouldn't be too difficult. Kids should take turns being "It." Setting time limits on being "It" is one way to rotate who's "It."

Frisbee Bowling: Any number of people can play this game, requiring very little skill. Set up ten paper cups, pyramid-style, several inches back from the edge of a table. From a distance of about twenty feet, players get three chances to knock as many of the cups as possible onto the floor by hitting them with a Frisbee. Each cup is worth one point. Each round can be considered a frame as in regular bowling; a game consists of ten frames. To keep the game moving, players can take turns throwing Frisbees, retrieving them, and restacking the paper cups. The highest number of total points determines the winner(s).

Frisbee on the Run: This game involves Frisbee throwing and a good deal of running. Begin by establishing two teams. Each team then positions half its members in a line at one end of the playing field and the other in a line directly opposite, at the other end of the field. Players must throw the team's Frisbee to their teammates across the field. After throwing it, they must run and tag the persons they have thrown to. The receiving players cannot be tagged unless they are behind the team line on their side of the field. So, if the first player throws the Frisbee inaccurately, the receiving player must go and get the Frisbee and run back to his or her original position before being tagged. After being tagged, that person can throw the Frisbee back the other way and repeat the process. The object of the game is to have the two halves of the team switch sides of the field. The first team to do so wins. You can lengthen or shorten the playing area depending on the skill of the group members.

Frisbee Stand-Off: For this event you will need one expendable Frisbee. The object is to have as many people as possible with their feet partially or wholly on the Frisbee or with their weight completely supported by people on the Frisbee. Designate teams and give them two minutes to practice. Each team then has one minute to get into position for the competition. At the end of the minute, a judge counts the total number of people "on" the Frisbee. The team with the most wins.

Frisbee Water Brigade: Another relay, this game involves carrying water in a Frisbee across an open space and filling up a quart container as quickly as possible. Teams begin lined up single file behind a starting line. Each team has a Frisbee of the same size, a large pan of water by its starting line, and a wide-mouth plastic quart container about twenty feet away. The object is to get the most water in the container as quickly as possible. Team members take turns carrying the Frisbee full of water and the team that fills the jar the most times in two minutes wins. Placing obstacles (chairs or boxes) in the path can add to the fun, but does require a bit more attention to safety concerns.

Killer Frisbee: Form a circle with people spaced so that there is plenty of room to move around in the middle, but not enough so that a player could remain in the center indefinitely. Place half the players in the middle and let the other half remain to form the surrounding circle. The object of the game for those in the middle is to avoid being hit by a Frisbee. Players in the outer circle throw the Frisbee(s). A single Frisbee is enough when the total group size is about ten; larger groups need two or three Frisbees to keep the game moving fast. Only hits below the shoulders count. Players that are hit must exchange places with whoever hit them.

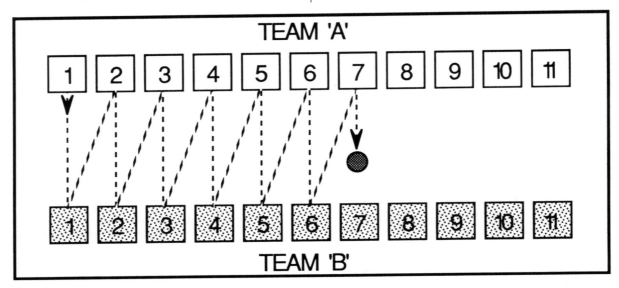

TEAM 'A'

1 2 3 4 5 6 7 8 9 10 11

1 2 3 4 5 6 7 8 9 10 11

TEAM 'B'

Team Toss Frisbee: Establish two teams and have them line up opposite each other about twenty feet apart. The first person on one team throws to the first person on the other team, who tosses the Frisbee back to the second person on the first team, who throws it back to the second person on the second team, and so on down the line (see diagram). The thrower's team scores a point if the catcher drops the Frisbee and the catcher's team scores a point if the thrower tosses the Frisbee beyond the reach of the catcher, who must keep his or her feet planted. Having a neutral judge will help settle disputes about whether a throw is or is not within reach. The game can be played to a certain score or until everyone has thrown the Frisbee four or five times.

Opposite-Hand Team Toss Frisbee: This is a variation of the game above. The rules are the same, but players must throw with their opposite hands. Right-handed players use their left hands; left-handed players use their right.

Revival

Here are some games that can be used to promote church attendance or to just have fun around the church for an evening.

Supply List:
Enough chairs for all members of the group, minus one

An offering plate for each team in "Pass the Plate"
A stack of old hymnbooks
Several Bibles
Rolled-up newspapers secured with rubber bands
One penny for everyone in your group

Lots of old keys that may fit doors around your church building
Slips of paper

Explanation:
Tell your group that in order for them to know how to attend a church service, they need to practice certain church-going skills. Select from the games and activities listed those ideas that would serve the needs and interests of the group.

Bible Characters Whack: This fun, fast-moving game will assure that your kids will not be left in the dark when the pastor talks about different Bible characters in the sermon next Sunday.

Have everyone sit in a circle. Each person takes the name of a Bible character (Job, Samson, Noah, and so on). Characters can be assigned or freely selected. One person is then chosen to stand in the middle of the circle with a rolled-up newspaper. This newspaper-wielder starts the game by calling out the name of a Bible character. The person who represents that character must stand up and call out the name of *another* character before the person in the middle is able to hit her or him on the head. The round continues until the player in the center actually whacks a character person before he or she calls out another name. The whackee then becomes the whacker and, accordingly, takes the rolled-up newspaper in hand and stands in the center of the circle. The following guidelines will help:
- Only the names of characters represented in the group can be called.
- Players cannot call out the character name represented by the person that just called them.
- Players cannot call out the name of the character of the person in the middle.
- Occasionally redistribute the charac-

ters among the players as action can get focused between the best-known characters.

Church Trivia: Divide the group into teams (or kids may compete individually) and give each a list of unusual things in the church to identify. Here is a sample list.
1. The name of the company that manufactured the church's fire extinguisher.
2. The number of steps in the baptistry.
3. The location of the first-aid kit.
4. The last word in a particular book in the church library.
5. The number of yellow lines painted on the parking lot.

The list should include twenty or so items. At a set signal, everyone tries to locate the various pieces of information required. If working in teams, the questions can be assigned to the different team members. The winner can be the first person or team to get all the answers, or the one with the most questions answered correctly.

Find a Seat: Just in case there is a standing-room-only crowd at the next church service, have your kids practice their skill with a game of "Musical Chairs."

Grab the Hymnal: There are not always enough hymnals to go around, so you have go to be quick! Play "Snatch the Bacon" using a hymnbook. Make sure it is an old one you do not mind getting damaged. The game is usually played outside, but will work inside if you have a large enough open area to be safe.

Divide the group into two teams and have them line up behind goal lines twenty to thirty feet apart. Each player is given a number, with players on both teams having corresponding numbers. The two teams are numbered from opposite ends of the line so that the same numbered players are positioned diagonally across from each other (except the two middle players, of course).

The leader calls out a number. The player on each team having that number must run to the center and try to grab the hymnal and return to his or her goal without being tagged by the other player. The more skilled players will run into the center and hover over the hymnal until their opponent is off guard and they can snatch it and run. Each successful return gains two points for the returning team. If tagged, the tagging team gets one point. Obviously, it pays to successfully grab the hymnal.

After each return or tag, the hymnal is placed back in the center, and another number is called. The game can be played for a certain number of points or for a set time period. The leader should try to call the numbers in a manner that creates suspense. All numbers should be included, but repeating a number now and then will keep all of the players alert.

Keys to the Kingdom: If you are in a big church, chances are good that there is a box or a desk drawer somewhere that has dozens of old keys in it, and nobody knows which key goes to which lock. Here is a solution to that problem. Pass out the keys to the kids in your group and give them fifteen minutes to see how many keys they can match up with a lock in the church. Whoever matches the most keys—or any key, for that matter—can be declared the winner!

Memory Verse: This activity is good practice for listening to the Scripture reading on Sunday. A variation of the "Gossip" game, a verse of Scripture is whispered around the group. Kids line up or sit in a circle. The verse is then whispered in the ear of the first person, who whispers it to the second, and so on down the line. The last person must quote the verse correctly. That doesn't always happen but the results are always entertaining.

Pass the Plate: Play this relay game to increase those offering plate passing skills. Have teams line up single file. Teams must have an equal number of players. Give the first players in each line an offering plate (or a reasonable substitute). They pass the plates over their heads to the next players in line. The second players pass it between their legs to the player behind them and so on. The offering plates continue to the end of each line, going over and under, and the team that finishes first wins.

Pew Races: This one is quite simple, but a fun game to play in the church sanctuary. Have all the contestants sit along the middle pew (equal distance from front and back). Give players a penny that they flip on a signal. If they get heads, they move forward a row; if they get tails, they go back a row. Play continues in this way, as quickly as players want to move, but they must flip in order to move each time. Players who reach the back row stay there until they get heads. The winner is the first one to reach the front row and then get heads. You may want to stipulate that players must either crawl under the pews or walk around them.

Sermon Cheers: Kids need to practice responding to good points in the sermon, right? Distribute on slips of paper words and phrases like "Amen," "Hallelujah," "Preach it, brother," "Glory," and other such enthusiastic responses. Have several slips for each expression. At a given signal, players must begin to yell out their expression and at the same time find everyone else in the room who is yelling out the same thing they are. The first group to get together wins.

The Great Pew Race: This game requires those bench-type pews that are found in many churches. Begin by dividing your group into small teams of three or four kids each. Have them all gather

at one end or the other of the church (whichever has the most room). At a given signal, the kids all at once dive under the first pew and must crawl all the way to the other end of the church and back, under the pews. The first team to have all its players return is the winner.

Scream Night

This is not a night for the quiet or shy—or, then again, maybe it is. The format is that all guests at the party must yell as loudly as possible each and every time they talk.

Supply List:
Handout—"Real Screamers" (one per person)
Tape recorder
Noise tape (see "Identify the Noise" game below)
Ice cream, various flavors
Various toppings
Serving spoons or scoops
Bowls
Napkins

Explanation:
Make sure to brief your sponsors ahead of time, especially about their primary role as examples of loud talking. As soon as the first kids arrive, the leaders start the shouting: "Hi, Mary!" or "Chris is here!" or "Look who just walked in!" Kids should get the point quickly. Select a number of games and activities to fit the mood.

End the evening with I SCREAM SUNDAES! Set up a long table with gallons of ice cream and a variety of toppings. Set out the dishes, dippers, spoons, and napkins, and let the kids make their own sundaes.

Real Screamers: The handout on the following page, "Real Screamers," can be used as a crowd breaker. Have the kids circulate and get as many signatures as possible. The kid or kids with the most signatures wins.

Barnyard: Ask everyone to sit down and to remain silent. Give each person a folded piece of paper with the name of one of the following six animals written on it: pig, horse, cow, chicken, duck, or dog. To ensure equal teams, assign the same animal name to every sixth person. Kids may not look at their papers until you give the signal. When all players have received a paper, tell them that in a moment you will turn out the lights and they must make the sound of the animal written on their papers. They are also to listen for other players making the same sound, to locate them in the dark, and link arms with them. Signal them to look at their papers and then turn out the lights.

Bedlam: See page 19.

Identify the Noise: Before this event, make a tape recording of a variety of noises. Have the group try to identify each noise on the tape.

Yeller Relay: Designate two teams. Members from each team try to yell instructions to each other from a distance of about twenty feet while the opposing team members yell and make as many distracting and contradictory noises as possible. For example, the first person runs to a point away from the team and receives from the leader an instruction like, "Run with your right hand up over your head." The player must yell that instruction to the next person in line until that person gets it and follows the instruction. Both teams are simultaneously trying to give and receive instructions while distracting the opposite team.

Gross Out Contest: Divide your group into teams with five to seven kids per team. Have each team try to come up with the most obnoxious, disgusting noise possible. Leaders determine the winners.

Skits:

The following skits—"Beautiful Bessie" and "Wild West Show"—require the involvement of the entire group making lots of noise. Choose one to do with your group.

BEAUTIFUL BESSIE

This skit can be done two ways. Either divide your entire group into nine small groups or have nine kids come to the front of the room to make the appropriate sound effects. The narrator reads the following story and whenever she or he gets to one of the words listed, whoever is assigned that word (one person or small group) yells out the proper sound effect. At the end of the story, when the narrator says, "Ride 'em Cowboy," the entire group is told to jump up and do all parts at the same time.

The Characters/Parts:

Rattlesnakes (hiss rattle, rattle; hiss rattle, rattle)
Cowboys (yippee)
Bessie (screams)
Love (coo-o-o-o)
Horses (stamp feet)
Cattle (moo-o-o-o)
Guns (bang, bang)
Wolves (yow-o-o-o)
Villain (ah-h-h-h-h-h-h-h-Hah-h-h-h)

The Story:

There once was a handsome **cowboy** named Bill Jones, who lived far, far out west on a great ranch. He spent most of his days riding the range on a fine black

Real Screamers!

Directions: Get as many signatures as possible. Ask people to sign their names after the statements that apply to them. The same person can sign no more than two places. Before they sign, they must prove it!

FIND SOMEONE WHO . . .

Screams at spiders. _____

Can hit the highest note. _____

Can YODEL LE DEHOOO. _____

Can whistle a happy tune. _____

Has the largest mouth. _____

Has the smallest mouth. _____

Can hit the lowest note. _____

Has the loudest scream. _____

Has the longest scream. _____

Has the funniest scream. _____

horse named Napoleon, and following his herds of bawling white-faced **cattle**.

On an adjoining ranch lived beautiful **Bessie** Brown with her aged parents. All the **cowboys loved Bessie**, but especially did the heart of the handsome Bill go pitter-patter when he looked into her eyes, which were limpid pools of darkness. The bold **villain**, Two-**Gun** Sam, also did feign to win the heart of beautiful **Bessie**, but she spurned his **love**.

One day **Bessie's** father and mother received a letter asking them to come to town at once, for the bad **villain** was about to foreclose on the mortgage to their ranch. Mr. Brown hitched up their **horses**, they put their **guns** in the wagon, Mrs. Brown placed her **rattlesnake** charm in her purse, and they drove away to town.

"Ahh—Haa," cried the bold **villain**, Two-**Gun** Sam, when they were out of sight, for he had forged the letter. "Now, I shall have the **love** of the Beautiful **Bessie**." So he rode his **horse** up to the house and shot both of his **guns**. Beautiful **Bessie** ran out of the house to see if someone had killed a **wolf** or a **rattlesnake**. When the girl saw Two-**Gun** Sam, she started to run for her **horse**. But the bold **villain** grabbed her by the wrist. "Ah, proud beauty," said he. "You shall be my wife and someday I shall own all of your father's **cattle**."

"Never," said **Bessie** "I do not **love** you."

"Then perhaps you would rather be taken to a den of **rattlesnakes** or eaten by the **wolves** or trampled by the **cattle**?"

"Ah, yes, anything rather than let you steal my **love** and take my father's **cattle**. Unhand me, you **villain**."

"Very well, proud beauty, to the **rattlesnakes** we go." And he put her on a **horse** and started to speed away.

Gun shots rang out, and two bullets went through the top of the bold **villain's** sombrero. "Stop—**villain**, **rattlesnake**, **wolf**!" It was the handsome **cowboy**, Bill Jones.

When Two-**Gun** Sam saw the **cowboy** he muttered to himself, "Curses, foiled again." He dropped Beautiful **Bessie** from his **horse**, threw his **gun** away, and started for the hills, where the **wolves** and **rattlesnakes** and **cattle** roam, for he knew he would never win the **love** of **Bessie** nor get her father's **cattle**.

The handsome **cowboy** looked into the eyes of the beautiful **Bessie**, which were still limpid pools of darkness, and they both forgot about the **wolves** and the **rattlesnakes** and the **villain** who wanted Mr. Brown's **cattle**.

Bessie thanked the handsome **cowboy** for rescuing her from the bold **villain** and she told Bill that she had been saving her **love** for him. So they rode off together on their **horses**.

Ride 'Em Cowboy!

WILD WEST SHOW

This skit can also be done one of two ways. You can select seven kids to come to the front and take the parts below, or have the entire group get into seven smaller groups, with each group taking one of the parts. The person (or group) assigned to each part makes the appropriate sound effect whenever that part's name comes up in the story, which is read by a narrator. The characters (or the groups) should try to overdo their parts and try to outdo each other. Every time one of the parts comes up in the story, the narrator should pause and allow time for the sound effect or motion. Give the winner (whoever does the best job) a prize.

The Characters/Parts:
The Cowboys ("whooppee!")

The Indians (an Indian yell with war dance)
The Women (scream)
The Horses (clippety-clop with hands and feet)
The Stagecoach (make circular motions with arms, like wheels)
The Rifles ("bang, bang")
The Bows and Arrows ("zip, zip," do the motions with hands)

The Story:

It was in the days of **stagecoaches** and **cowboys** and **Indians**. Alkali Ike, Dippy Dick, and Pony Pete were three courageous **cowboys**. When the **stagecoach** left for Rainbow's End they were aboard, as were also two **women**, Salty Sal and a doll-faced blonde. The **stagecoach** was drawn by three handsome **horses** and it left Dead End exactly on time.

The most dangerous part of the journey was the pass known as Gory Gulch. As the **stagecoach** neared this spot, it could be noticed that the **women** were a bit nervous and the **cowboys** were alert, fingering their **rifles** as if to be ready for any emergency. Even the **horses** seemed to sense the danger.

Sure enough, just as the **stagecoach** entered the Gulch, there sounded the blood-curdling war cry of the **Indians**. Mounted on **horses**, they came riding wildly toward the **stagecoach**, aiming their **bows and arrows**. The **cowboys** took aim with their **rifles** and fired. The **women** screamed. The **horses** pranced nervously. The **Indians** shot their **bows and arrows**. The **cowboys** aimed their **rifles** again, this time shooting with more deadly effect. The leading brave fell and the **Indians** turned their **horses** and fled, leaving their **bows and arrows** behind. The **women** fainted. The **cowboys** shot one more volley from their **rifles**, just for luck. The driver urged on the **horses**, and the **stagecoach** sped down the trail.

Taffy Pull

If you are looking for an event to help build a sense of community, this hands-on activity is great. An old-fashioned taffy pull will keep kids busy for up to three hours and provide lots of edible fun.

Supply List:

A large sauce pan
A small sauce pan (for dissolving gelatin)
A pie tin
1 stick of butter
2 rolls of waxed paper
Knife

Taffy Ingredients:

2 pounds granulated sugar (4 cups)
2 cups light corn syrup
2 cups sweetened condensed milk
Paraffin wax, the size of a walnut
1 tablespoon Knox gelatin
1 cup warm to hot water

CAUTION

The mixture will be extremely hot. Have plenty of adult supervision on hand. Allow the mixture to cool completely (inside as well as on the surface) before allowing kids to handle it. Also, make sure all participants have thoroughly washed their hands.

Explanation:

The following "Pulling" games from Chapter Two will get your group in the mood to pull taffy. Choose two or three to play before you begin to pull the taffy.

Because these games involve pulling, be sure to appoint Safety Guards.

- Dr. Tangle on page 21
- Line Pull on page 24
- Drop the Keys on page 20
- Crack the Whip on page 19
- Pull Off on page 26

Directions for Taffy: While those in the kitchen are making taffy, have the rest of the group cut waxed paper into three-quarter-inch squares.

Dissolve one tablespoon Knox gelatin in one cup warm to hot water. Mix sugar, corn syrup, milk, and paraffin over medium heat in a large saucepan. Let the mixture come to a boil (this will take approximately twenty to thirty minutes), then add the dissolved gelatin. Stir continuously until the mixture boils again. Turn heat back to low. The mixture is ready when a few drops in cold water form a soft ball. It should look dark yellow and bubbly. Have an adult pour the mixture into a greased pie pan. Let it cool in the refrigerator for fifteen to thirty minutes.

When the taffy has cooled and is hard enough to pull, cut the mixture in half. Have kids who will be pulling the taffy remove all jewelry and butter their hands. Have two people pull each half using a hand-over-hand, dog paddle motion. It will take at least twenty to thirty minutes of pulling before the taffy can be cut and wrapped. The taffy will change to a lighter color as it is pulled. When this happens, cut it into small sections. Lay these on a table and cut into half-inch strips. Have everyone wrap the taffy pieces.

This recipe makes approximately two and a half pounds. The mixture may be doubled or tripled as needed.

CHAPTER

8

Ready-to-Use Growth Games

Learning games are great ways for kids to have fun while discovering more about God's Word and the Christian life. The selection of games provided here can help kids to consider their own needs for Christian growth.

Bible-Book Guess

This simple game is a fun way for your kids to review the books of the Bible. Photocopy pages 99 through 102. Cut out each of the squares and scramble them in a box or a basket. Divide the group into two teams. Kids take turns drawing cards; then they name the book immediately preceding or following the book they have drawn. You decide whether to have them name the preceding or following book, or you can give them the choice. A wrong answer sends the card back into the box. When the box is empty, the team with the most cards wins. (See page 103 for an answer sheet to check kids' answers.)

Gospel Twenty Questions

Divide the group into two teams. Photocopy pages 104 and 105 and then cut them into individual cards, each card with the name of a Bible character written on it. Place the cards in a box or basket. One person from each team must draw a card. The two players then huddle with their teammates for one to two minutes to find out as much as possible about the person whose name they have drawn. They should not let the opposing team know who it is.

Teams then take turns asking each other a "yes/no" question about the identity of the opposing team's character. After each question, they can make one guess as to who it is. Questions can be answered only by the player who drew the name, but teammates can coach their players. The only answers that can be given are "yes," "no," or "I don't know." If the player does not know the answer, or if the answer given is wrong, the opposing team gets to ask another question. A leader should be the judge as to whether an answer is right or wrong. The team that guesses the correct character first wins a point for that round. The highest score after ten rounds wins. Each round should involve a different pair of players.

Some sample questions: Is this character in the Gospels? Is this character human (as opposed to God, angels, devils, or animals)? Is this character a woman? Is this character a political leader? You might want to have someone from each team record the answers—it is easy to forget in the excitement of the moment!

Name That Scripture

This game is a spin-off from the old TV show *Name That Tune*. It can be used at a meeting or social to test your group's knowledge of familiar Bible passages.

Divide your group into two teams. The two teams position themselves on opposite sides of the room. A leader stands in the middle with a list of well-known verses from the Bible. One such list can be photocopied from page 106, or you can prepare a list of your own.

The two teams send out one person at a time to compete. These team representatives then "bid" for the first verse. Bids are made in terms of how many words the player claims to need in order to guess the verse. The first bidder might say something like, "I can name that Scripture in six words!" The other player then can say, "I can name that Scripture in five words!"—if he or she thinks it's possible. The bidding continues until one player stops. The idea is to stop at some point where the other player—if he or she wins the bid—will be unable to complete the verse, or to stop at a point where one player will be able to say the verse if he or she wins the bidding.

Once the bidding is done, the leader provides the first words of the verse, as many as were bid. The player who won the bid must then attempt to correctly complete the verse. If successful, the team gets a point. If unsuccessful, the opposing player gets an additional word and the opportunity to complete the verse. If successful, he or she gets the point. In other words, whoever wins the bidding gets first crack at winning the point. If the second player does not complete the verse correctly, then it goes back to the first player with an additional word, and so on.

To make the game a bit more risky, the following rules can be added:

• If a player wins the bid but cannot complete the verse correctly, the

opposing player gets *two* points for quoting the correct verse.
- The second player may consult with

his or her team before answering. What this does is make sure that the bidding is taken seriously.

Old Testament-New Testament

Here is a good Bible game for younger kids. Have everyone sit in a circle. Choose someone to be "It," who then sits in the middle. "It" tosses a small bean bag to someone in the circle and calls out either "Old Testament" or "New Testament." The person receiving the bag must respond appropriately with either the name of an Old or New Testament book before "It" can count to ten. If the player responds correctly, "It" must try again. If the person with the bag responds incorrectly or is too slow in giving the correct answer, he or she becomes the new "It." The game becomes more difficult as it goes along

because each book of the Bible may be used only once.

The game can be varied: when the person who is "It" tosses the bag to someone and calls out the name of a book of the Bible, the person receiving the bag must then correctly respond either "New Testament" or "Old Testament" before "It" can count to ten. In this version, "It" can also call out the name of a nonexistent book of the Bible (e.g., First Peaches), at which time the person with the bag should respond by saying, "No Testament."

Page 103 can be photocopied to use as a sheet to record and check answers.

Peter-Paul Basketball

Visit any classroom and you will witness kids' love of tossing wadded-up papers into the trash can ten feet away. This indoor game perfects that very skill and prepares kids for a general New Testament study at the same time.

Before the meeting you (and some helpers) should prepare three sheets of paper for each participant, one with *Jesus* written on it, one with the name *Peter*, and one with the name *Paul*. To accommodate two teams, half the trios should be one color, and the other half another color. Then crumple up all the sheets into balls and bag them in six separate bags—the Paul balls of one color in one, the Paul balls of the other

color in another. Also before the meeting, photocopy the Scripture addresses of the statements of Jesus, Peter, and Paul that can be found on the page 107.

At the meeting divide the group into two teams. Give each person on a team a Jesus, a Peter, and a Paul ball of the same color. Everyone should have three wadded-up paper balls. The members of one team line up along a free-throw line about eight feet away from a trash can. A leader then reads one of the Scripture statements, leaving out the names of Jesus, Peter, and Paul if they appear in the passage. The team members listen as the statements are read, decide individually within ten seconds who said it, and then throw the appropriate wad. The team is awarded as many points as there are correct wads in the trash can.

Subtract points if teammates give the answers to each other or if they step over the line as they throw. Wads are retrieved by the shooting team, and then the other team lines up to take its turn.

Bible-Book Guess

Genesis	2 Samuel
Exodus	1 Kings
Leviticus	2 Kings
Numbers	1 Chronicles
Deuteronomy	2 Chronicles
Joshua	Ezra
Judges	Nehemiah
Ruth	Esther
1 Samuel	Job

Bible-Book Guess

Psalms	Hosea
Proverbs	Joel
Ecclesiastes	Amos
Song of Songs	Obadiah
Isaiah	Jonah
Jeremiah	Micah
Lamentations	Nahum
Ezekiel	Habakkuk
Daniel	Zephaniah

Bible-Book Guess

Haggai	1 Corinthians
Zechariah	2 Corinthians
Malachi	Galatians
Matthew	Ephesians
Mark	Philippians
Luke	Colossians
John	1 Thessalonians
Acts	2 Thessalonians
Romans	1 Timothy

Bible-Book Guess

2 Timothy	2 Peter
Titus	1 John
Philemon	2 John
Hebrews	3 John
James	Jude
1 Peter	Revelation

Bible-Book Guess Answer Sheet

OLD TESTAMENT BOOKS
Genesis
Exodus
Leviticus
Numbers
Deuteronomy
Joshua
Judges
Ruth
1 Samuel
2 Samuel
1 Kings
2 Kings
1 Chronicles
2 Chronicles
Ezra
Nehemiah
Esther
Job
Psalms
Proverbs
Ecclesiastes
Song of Songs
Isaiah
Jeremiah
Lamentations
Ezekiel
Daniel
Hosea
Joel
Amos
Obadiah
Jonah
Micah
Nahum
Habakkuk
Zephaniah
Haggai
Zechariah
Malachi

NEW TESTAMENT BOOKS
Matthew
Mark
Luke
John
Acts
Romans
1 Corinthians
2 Corinthians
Galatians
Ephesians
Philippians
Colossians
1 Thessalonians
2 Thessalonians
1 Timothy
2 Timothy
Titus
Philemon
Hebrews
James
1 Peter
2 Peter
1 John
2 John
3 John
Jude
Revelation

Gospel Twenty Questions

Mary, Christ's Mother Matthew 1:18-25 Luke 1:26-38 John 1:1-18	**John the Baptist** Matthew 3:1-17 Luke 3:1-20 John 1:6-34
Joseph, Christ's Earthly Father John 6:22-59 Mark 6:1-6 Matthew 2:13-15, 19-23	**Pharisees** Mark 2:23-3:30 Luke 11:37-12:15; 13:31-14:15
The Innkeeper Luke 2:1-20	**Tax Collectors** Mark 2:13-20 Luke 5:27-32
The Shepherds Luke 2:1-20	**Twelve Disciples** Matthew 10:1-11:1
Magi Matthew 2:1-18	**Jesus' Family** Luke 8:19-21 Mark 3:31-35 John 7:1-9
Jesus, the Child Luke 2:41-52	**Wise and Foolish Builders** Matthew 7:24-27

Gospel Twenty Questions

Prodigal Son Luke 15:1-24	**Lazarus, the Beggar** Luke 16:19-17:6
Nicodemus John 3:1-16; 7:50-53; 19:39-42	**Judas** Matthew 27:3-10 Luke 22:1-6 John 12:1-8; 13:21-35
Woman at the Well John 4:1-30	**Man with Leprosy** Matthew 8:1-4 Mark 1:40-45
Martha and Mary Luke 10:38-42 John 11:1-5	**Pilate** Mark 15:1-15 Luke 23:1-7, 11-25 John 18:28-19:16
Zacchaeus Luke 19:1-10	**Lazarus** John 11:1-44
The Good Samaritan Luke 10:30-37	**Risen Jesus** Matthew 28:16-20 Luke 24:13-53 John 20:10-30

Name That Scripture

Genesis 1:1
Genesis 15:6
Exodus 4:12
Numbers 6:24-26
Deuteronomy 4:35
Joshua 24:15b
1 Samuel 16:7c
Psalm 37:4
Psalm 51:2
Psalm 67:1
Psalm 103:12
Psalm 106:1
Psalm 118:6
Psalm 128:1
Proverbs 3:5
Proverbs 3:6
Ecclesiastes 3:1
Ecclesiastes 12:1a
Isaiah 26:3
Isaiah 43:25
Jeremiah 31:3
Nahum 1:7
Matthew 5:16
Matthew 6:20
Matthew 7:1
Matthew 28:19
Mark 12:30
Mark 12:31
Luke 1:37
Luke 23:34

John 3:16
John 3:17
John 5:24
John 10:30
John 11:35
John 13:34
John 14:6
Acts 1:8
Romans 3:23
Romans 5:1
Romans 5:8
Romans 8:1
Romans 8:28
Romans 10:13
Romans 12:1
Romans 12:2
1 Corinthians 3:16
1 Corinthians 10:24
1 Corinthians 15:57
Galatians 5:16
Galatians 5:22-23
Galatians 5:25
Ephesians 1:7
Ephesians 2:8
Ephesians 2:10
Ephesians 4:3
Ephesians 4:29
Ephesians 5:1
Ephesians 5:15
Ephesians 6:1

Philippians 1:6
Philippians 2:11
Philippians 3:7
Philippians 4:6
Philippians 4:13
1 Thessalonians 5:16
1 Thessalonians 5:17
1 Thessalonians 5:18
1 Thessalonians 5:22
2 Thessalonians 2:16-17
1 Timothy 4:12
1 Timothy 6:6
2 Timothy 1:7
2 Timothy 2:15
2 Timothy 2:22
2 Timothy 3:16
Hebrews 9:27
James 1:13
James 1:22
James 4:7
James 4:8
1 Peter 5:7
1 John 1:9
1 John 2:15
1 John 2:16
1 John 2:17
1 John 4:11
1 John 5:3
2 John 6
Revelation 3:20

Peter-Paul Basketball

Jesus	Peter	Paul
Matthew 4:17	Matthew 14:28	Acts 15:36
Matthew 5:16	Matthew 16:16	Acts 17:22, 24
Matthew 6:19-21	Matthew 18:21	Romans 1:16
Matthew 7:1-2	Matthew 26:33	Romans 3:22-24
Matthew 7:13-14	Matthew 26:35	Romans 5:8
Matthew 9:37-38	Mark 8:29b	Romans 8:28
Matthew 14:27	Mark 10:28	Romans 12:2
Matthew 16:24	John 6:68-69	1 Corinthians 10:24
Mark 1:17	John 13:8	1 Corinthians 13:4-8
Mark 2:17	John 13:37	1 Corinthians 15:57
Mark 8:29a	John 21:17c	2 Corinthians 9:6-7
Mark 12:30-31	Acts 2:38	Galatians 2:20
Mark 15:34b	Acts 3:6	Galatians 5:22-23
Mark 16:15	Acts 10:34	Galatians 6:7
Luke 6:27	1 Peter 1:14	Ephesians 2:8
Luke 9:23	1 Peter 1:18-19	Ephesians 3:20
Luke 11:2-4	1 Peter 1:22	Ephesians 5:1
Luke 12:22	1 Peter 2:9	Ephesians 6:10-11
Luke 18:16	1 Peter 2:12	Philippians 2:14-15
John 3:16	1 Peter 2:16	Philippians 4:13
John 5:24	1 Peter 2:11	Colossians 3:13
John 6:35	1 Peter 4:8	Colossians 3:20
John 6:70	1 Peter 5:7	1 Thessalonians 4:17
John 7:7	1 Peter 5:8	1 Thessalonians 5:15
John 8:12b	2 Peter 1:5-7	2 Thessalonians 2:16-17
John 8:58	2 Peter 1:16	1 Timothy 2:1
John 11:25	2 Peter 3:3	2 Timothy 2:22
John 13:10	2 Peter 3:8	2 Timothy 3:16
John 13:34	2 Peter 3:9	Titus 3:4-5
John 14:1	2 Peter 3:13	Philemon 7